MARVEL
VEHICLES

OWNER'S WORKSHOP MANUAL

MARVEL
VEHICLES

OWNER'S WORKSHOP MANUAL

BY ALEX IRVINE

CONTENTS

IF YOU'RE READING THIS, you probably already know who I am, but just in case—because I am nothing if not polite—I'll tell you. It's my job to run the Strategic Homeland Intervention and Enforcement Logistics Division, better known as S.H.I.E.L.D. I was asked to write the introduction to this book, and once I got through wondering whether they'd meant to call some other Nick Fury—I've been a lot of things, but nobody ever called me a writer—I got down to it. So here I am wearing my public-face-of-S.H.I.E.L.D. hat and telling you why this book in your hands is unlike anything else you've ever had a chance to read.

S.H.I.E.L.D., as you might know, is tasked with defending the freedoms of every living human being—and friendly aliens, too. One of those freedoms is the liberty to read this book. It's got all kinds of information that was classified six months ago. Hell, some of it was classified six days ago. But now it's in this book because the free exchange of information is part of what we're fighting for.

This book gives you a look inside the most amazing wheels and wings the human mind has ever created. You see Helicarriers in the sky once in a while, or a Blackbird overhead. Ever wonder what the inside looks like? Now you're going to know. You saw video of when Thanos showed up in his ship over New York not too long ago; now you're going to get a look inside that ship and learn a little about how it works.

S.H.I.E.L.D. had the full cooperation of the Avengers and some of Earth's great heroes when we were putting together this book. The Guardians of the Galaxy pitched in with a tour of their new ship. We even got Frank Castle to give us a look inside his Battle Van. You better believe that's never happened before. There's also plenty of information about enemy vehicles, too. If Galactus ever makes another pass by Earth, you'll be able to look up at the sky and tell whether he's flying Taa II or his Star Sphere.

And along with the cutaway drawings and the tech specs, you'll hear stories from the heroes who have operated these vehicles—or fought against them. Remember Norman Osborn's H.A.M.M.E.R. Helicarrier, the big black one Tony Stark wrecked during the siege of Asgard? That was an imposing piece of hardware, and thanks to Stark you're about to read the inside story of how it went up in flames. Not all of you have met Rocket Raccoon yet, but most of you will real soon. He's got stories from his Ranger days—tied to some of the old Guardians of the Galaxy ships— that you'll want to hear. Tell your friends. Tell your kids. These are the planes and ships and cars that helped make those stories happen.

One of the most potent weapons in the hands of our enemies is misinformation. S.H.I.E.L.D. has been the target of a number of misinformation campaigns, and this book is in some ways a defense against those attacks. Because one thing that separates S.H.I.E.L.D. from Hydra or A.I.M. or the Hellfire Club is that S.H.I.E.L.D. is, essentially, crowdsourced. We see potential and we bring it in. We try to put people in the right places in our organization where they'll do the most good, because our mission is to protect the people of Earth from those who would menace their lives and freedom. Call this book a recruiting effort if you will, or a public relations effort. That's fine. Call it whatever you want, as long as you read it.

You might never pilot a Quinjet or take a ride on the Goblin Glider, but after you turn these pages, you'll know more about what it's like. And if that inspires you to get yourself in shape and take a S.H.I.E.L.D. training course? So much the better. We're always looking.

NICK FURY

X-VEHICLES

- BLACKBIRD
- DOVE
- STRATOJET
- X-COPTER

BLACKBIRD

DESCRIPTION AND OPERATIONAL HISTORY

The X-Jet, or Blackbird, is a high-altitude, high-speed reconnaissance and light combat aircraft. Continuously modified over the five decades of its service life, the Blackbird has existed in numerous models designed for general use as well as specific operational tasks such as search and rescue.

THE FIRST BLACKBIRD

There have been several generations of the Blackbird. The first was a custom S.H.I.E.L.D. design given the designation RS-150. This craft was a successor to the destroyed Stratojet and symbolized a new era of cooperation between the X-Men, S.H.I.E.L.D., and the Avengers. Built using the fundamental fuselage structure of a classified military surveillance prototype, the RS-150 was powered by twin J58-class turbojets, with afterburner capabilities that boosted the aircraft's maximum speed to Mach 3.5 at 80,000 feet. This was largely in line with the existing capabilities of the prototype. S.H.I.E.L.D. modifications to the design expanded crew capacity and introduced new weaponry. A further modification, critical to the Blackbird's usefulness for the X-Men, was the retrofitting of vertical takeoff and landing (VTOL) capability. This innovation necessitated a number of changes to the prototypes's aeronautical profile, resulting in the RS-150 being unique when compared to military aircraft models.

BELOW: In most recent models, the Blackbird's VTOL capability is accomplished without standard landing gear. Instead, a single retractable landing arm is deployed, as seen in this anti-Sentinel mission. OPPOSITE: The Blackbird's VTOL capability also allows for midair takeoff and landing, as here where the aircraft is seen redeploying from a S.H.I.E.L.D. Helicarrier.

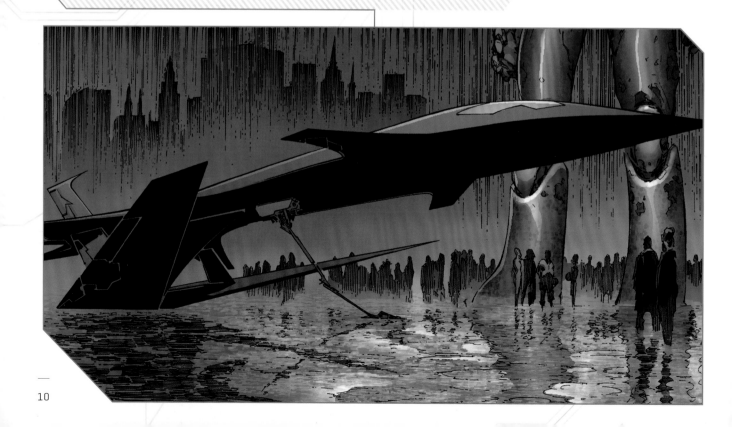

THROTTLE FIRE-WALLED, THE MODIFIED SR-71 BLACKBIRD SKIMS THE TREELINE AT A BARE TWENTY FEET, ITS MACH 4 SONIC BOOMS THUNDERING THROUGH THE NARROW PASSES LIKE THE THUNDER OF THOR HIMSELF...

IT'S A MAD, DESPERATE GAMBLE CYCLOPS TRIES...

... AND IS REBORN, THE LIFTING BODY RISING SWIFTLY, SURELY, FROM THE ASHES OF ITS DEAD PARENT.

FHWOOM!

ABOVE: From its first prototype, the Blackbird was designed for maximum maneuverability in the thicker air of low altitudes while maintaining the stratospheric flight ceiling of the SR-71.
OPPOSITE BOTTOM: Recent iterations of command-and-control systems include holographic heads-up displays that automatically prioritize mission-critical flight and combat information.

THE SECOND GENERATION

The second Blackbird took advantage of new aeronautical advances and used the basic fuselage of existing military spy planes, which were themselves developmental advances on the post–World War II reconnaissance aircraft that contributed elements to the original RS-150. It was assembled at a top-secret facility in cooperation with several defense contractors and then given a number of upgrades and augmentations by the X-Men. The original SR-71 seated only two crew members, but the X-Men's version could carry seven. It was also capable of Mach 4 speeds, much faster than the regular model.

The first Blackbird of this generation was destroyed when the X-Men went after Count Nefaria, who shot it down after commandeering the NORAD missile command center in Colorado. The X-Men escaped in a detachable pod called a lifting body, but that escape was short-lived, as Nefaria disintegrated the lifting body, too.

Blackbirds were equipped with a variety of weapons systems, but resourceful members of the team sometimes put them to use in unexpected ways, as when a young Kitty Pryde killed an N'Garai demon with the jet's afterburners. Twin exhaust ports, each venting 20,000 kilograms of thrust, were more than enough to do the job.

After the Blackbird's destruction, another was built and quickly put into service. It survived an emergency water landing when it mistakenly flew over Magneto's Caribbean hideaway and into a damping field that crippled its electronic systems, causing it to crash.

Like the Stratojet sunk during the battle on Krakoa, the Blackbird featured a sealed fuselage and cockpit that protected it from damage despite its immersion in salt water.

THIRD GENERATION

Although constructed using the same fuselage and frame as previous Blackbirds, the next-generation version added a number of advances derived from the technology of the alien Shi'ar. This redesign was overseen by the mutant technological savant known as Forge.

Among the advances Forge incorporated into this new design were a cloaking device and a version of Cerebro's mutant-detection software. The engines were retooled using Shi'ar technology as well, abandoning the classic turbine-intake engine for a ramjet design that increased thrust and range; this jet could reach Mach 4.2 at 120,000 feet, and Mach 2.3 in the denser air at sea level. Its operational range approached 13,000 miles empty and 8,000 miles with a full crew, depending on airspeed and atmospheric conditions, and its service ceiling was 230,000 feet. Combined crew and passenger capacity was seven, with an ejectable escape pod built into the fuselage anterior of the cockpit. A number of examples of this iteration of the Blackbird were built and housed in a dedicated hangar.

CYCLOPS

" FIRST TEAM MEMBER WE EVER LOST WAS DURING THAT FIGHT AGAINST NEFARIA. NEFARIA TOOK OFF IN A GETAWAY PLANE WITH THUNDERBIRD HANGING ONTO THE OUTSIDE OF THE JET, TEARING HIS WAY IN. HE WASN'T GOING TO LET NEFARIA GO, AND HE WAS ALSO DETERMINED TO PROVE THAT HE BELONGED IN THE TEAM. THE JET BLEW UP AND NEFARIA TELEPORTED HIMSELF AWAY . . . THUNDERBIRD DIDN'T MAKE IT. "

BLACKBIRD

X5, STANDARD MODEL "X-JET"

COMMUNICATIONS, SURVEILLANCE, FLIGHT CONTROL, FIRE CONTROL INSTRUMENTATION CONSOLE

7-SEAT PASSENGER/CREW CABIN

SURVEILLANCE INSTRUMENTATION, CABIN LIFE-SUPPORT MECHANISMS, LANDING GEAR HOUSING

MULTISPECTRAL RADAR/RADIO/IMAGING PROCESSING EQUIPMENT

ACTIVE RADAR DISH, COMMUNICATIONS SATELLITE INTERFACE

ADJUSTABLE THRUSTER NOZZLE

TWIN TURBOJETS, WITH DEFLECTOR THRUST
SHIELDS FOR VTOL CAPABILITY

WING HOUSING MULTIPLE REDUNDANT
FUEL-DELIVERY SYSTEMS

SHI'AR-DERIVED RAMJET ENGINE
BASED ON J-58 DESIGN

ROTOR CONE FOR MAXIMUM AIR COMPRESSION

FUEL CELLS, ELECTRONICS, CREW SUPPLIES,
INTERNAL WEAPON SYSTEMS HOUSINGS

BLACKBIRD: X5 SPECS & FEATURES

CREW CAPACITY	7 standard, varies with specific models
FUSELAGE LENGTH	88 feet, 4 inches standard; varies with instrument packages
WINGSPAN	62 feet, 6 inches; wings fold for VTOL on some models
PROPULSION	Twin J-58 turbojets, enhanced with Shi'ar ramjet technology; additional pair of center-mounted turbojets for additional thrust and VTOL control
FLIGHT CEILING	230,000 feet standard
MAXIMUM AIRSPEED	Mach 4.2 at 130,000 feet

ABOVE: Among the Blackbirds destroyed in action was this model, seen here falling victim to Xorn.
OPPOSITE TOP: The Blackbird's VTOL package makes it possible to land the vehicle in extremely tight spaces and on broken or uneven ground.
OPPOSITE BOTTOM: This Blackbird was created by the X-Men's enemy Kaga, with insectile flourishes reflecting Kaga's alliance with the alien Brood. The X-Men commandeered it and turned it against Kaga and his creations.

FOURTH GENERATION

Beast retooled the Blackbirds after Cerebro achieved sentience and went rogue. A new variation on Cerebro, known as Cerebra, was integrated into this new generation of planes. The craft also featured an X designed across the top of the fuselage, representing the new X-Corporation.

FIFTH GENERATION

Following the collapse of X-Corporation and the destruction of Xavier's mansion by Xorn, Cyclops commissioned Angel to build updated Blackbirds and designed an underground hangar and maintenance facility as part of their headquarters.

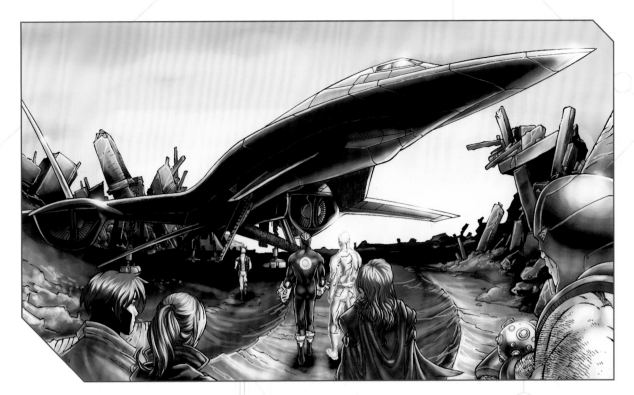

This newest generation of Blackbirds is equipped with a variety of defense and weapons systems, including automatic laser batteries and concussion missiles. The planes also maintain Forge's previous Shi'ar-derived enhancements, including sensor arrays, engine components, and deep space–ready cabin life-support systems. Specific variants have also been adapted for the use of individual X-Men. For example, Cyclops has used a Blackbird with a ruby-quartz windshield that channels his optic blasts.

A Blackbird known as X2 got its shakedown cruise in a mission against an alien-Sentinel hybrid in San Francisco. Designed for rescue operations, this version carried no offensive weaponry, but, despite this limitation, Beast managed to take down the hybrid. The X2 was destroyed soon after, having enjoyed a short operational life, even by Blackbird standards.

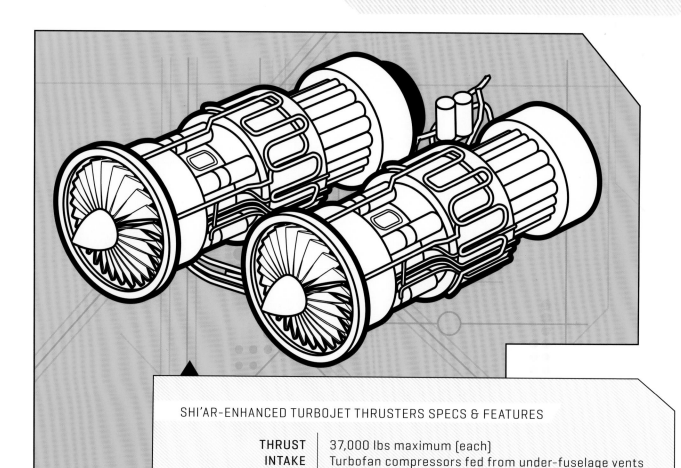

SHI'AR-ENHANCED TURBOJET THRUSTERS SPECS & FEATURES

THRUST	37,000 lbs maximum (each)
INTAKE	Turbofan compressors fed from under-fuselage vents
DEFLECTORS	Twin deflector shields and ducts, permitting vertical takeoff and landing independent of wing engine thrust
CONTROL	Automatic adjustment related to wing engine thrust capacity for increased flight stability
SECONDARY POWER	Standby solid fuel reserve with separate feed

ABOVE: The thrust controls on the newer generations of the Blackbird permit precision flying unique among fixed-wing aircraft. Here the Blackbird navigates crowded urban airspace in a combat environment.

OPPOSITE TOP: The Blackbird's armament systems are typically housed within the fuselage, improving aerodynamic efficiency and flight stability.

DOVE

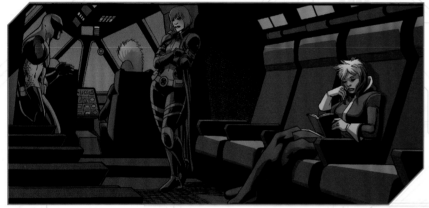

DOVE SPECS & FEATURES

CREW CAPACITY 8

FUSELAGE MATERIAL Unique multi-layer alloy designed to absorb and ablate incoming energy blasts as well as kinetic weaponry

TOP SPEED Mach 4 at 56,000 feet; slightly slower at lower altitudes

ENGINES Twin hot-inlet ramjets, with variable intakes that double as lift adjusters, each generating 42,000 pounds of thrust

OPERATIONAL RANGE 4,600 miles with full crew complement

FLIGHT CEILING Unknown; tested to 146,000 feet

BEAST

IT'S CERTAINLY NOT EVERY DAY YOU GET TO COLLABORATE WITH TWO OTHER VERSIONS OF YOURSELF ON A DREAM PROJECT, BUT THAT'S EXACTLY HOW THE DOVE CAME INTO BEING. THANKS TO THE VARIOUS SPATIO-TEMPORAL LOOPS OBSERVED DURING WHAT WE CALLED THE BATTLE OF THE ATOM, I AND TWO OF MY OTHER SELVES WERE ABLE TO PUT OUR COLLECTIVE HEADS TOGETHER AND BUILD A NEW JET. IT'S SMALLER THAN THE BLACKBIRD, MORE NIMBLE IN THE AIR—AND, AS WE DISCOVERED WHILE PURSUING THE YOUNG RUNAWAYS SCOTT AND JEAN—IT CAN HANDLE SCOTT'S OPTIC BLASTS WITHOUT MUCH TROUBLE. THE DOVE IS A STANDOUT EXAMPLE OF AERONAUTICAL INGENUITY. CAN'T IMAGINE WHAT TOOK ME SO LONG TO GET AROUND TO BUILDING IT. ASK MY OLDER SELF, PERHAPS.

TOP LEFT: The Dove is smaller than the Blackbird but features a similar fuselage profile.

TOP RIGHT: Front stabilizers and divided intake and thruster assemblies increase the Dove's in-flight maneuverability.

MIDDLE LEFT: The Dove's passenger cabin can accommodate six people, with two more in the cockpit.

STRATOJET

CYCLOPS

"BEFORE WE HAD THE BLACKBIRD, THE STRATOJET WAS THE X-MEN'S PRIMARY MEANS OF GROUP AIR TRANSPORT. IT WAS FAST, AND ITS VERTICAL TAKEOFF AND LANDING CAPABILITIES CAME IN HANDY DURING OPERATIONS WHERE WE COULDN'T BRING IN A REGULAR PLANE. IT WAS ALSO AIRTIGHT FOR HIGH-ALTITUDE OPERATION, AND THAT LITTLE FEATURE SAVED OUR BACON WHEN WE TANGLED WITH THE SENTIENT ISLAND OF KRAKOA. POLARIS THREW THE ISLAND INTO SPACE TO SAVE OUR LIVES, BUT WE WERE LEFT TREADING WATER AND WONDERING WHAT TO DO NEXT. THEN THE STRATOJET BOBBED RIGHT UP TO THE SURFACE NEARBY. IT HAD BEEN THROWN CLEAR IN THE UPHEAVAL, AND ALL WE HAD TO DO WAS CLIMB ABOARD AND HEAD HOME."

STRATOJET SPECS & FEATURES

CREW CAPACITY	6
ENGINES	Twin turbojets, proprietary design, each generating 28,000 pounds of thrust
OPERATIONAL RANGE	4,400 miles with full crew complement; can be refueled midair
FLIGHT CEILING	77,000 feet
OTHER FEATURES	Escape hatches on top and bottom of fuselage; airtight construction providing life support and buoyancy

LEFT: The Stratojet introduced the split tail design that became a standard feature of later X-Planes from the Blackbird to the Dove.

BELOW: The Stratojet's advanced engine design and innovative fuselage material made it perhaps the fastest aircraft of its time.

X-COPTER

THIS PAGE: The X-Copter's cockpit combines excellent field of vision with compact flight control and instrument systems.

X-COPTER SPECS & FEATURES

CREW CAPACITY	2
ENGINE	Main rotor: single turbine; stabilizing counter-torque engines in place of tail rotor situated on either side of fuselage
ROTOR	Fully articulated, 4 blades, rotational speed 467 rpm
RANGE	523 miles with full crew
TOP SPEED	144 miles per hour
FLIGHT CEILING	10,000 feet

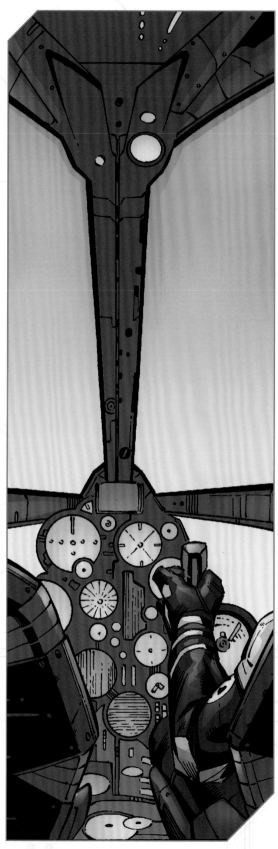

CYCLOPS

ABOVE: Three different views of the X-Copter in flight demonstrate its retractable landing gear and fuselage-mounted turbo intakes.

"PROFESSOR XAVIER GOT THE X-COPTER FOR THE TEAM RIGHT AFTER WE ALL CAME TOGETHER. I WAS THE FIRST ONE WHO LEARNED HOW TO FLY IT. THIS WAS RIGHT AROUND THE TIME THE ORIGINAL BROTHERHOOD OF EVIL MUTANTS WAS BREAKING UP. WE PUT IT TO GOOD USE—AND NOT ALWAYS JUST TO FLY. ONCE, WHEN WE WERE TANGLING WITH JUGGERNAUT, BEAST TIPPED IT AT AN ANGLE SO WE COULD USE ITS ROTOR BLADES AS A BARRIER. EVEN JUGGERNAUT DIDN'T SEEM SO UNSTOPPABLE WHEN HE HAD TO WALK THROUGH ROTORS SPINNING AT 5000 RPM. ONCE WE HAD THE STRATOJET AND THEN THE BLACKBIRD, WE DIDN'T USE THE X-COPTER AS MUCH. I REMEMBER USING IT TO FERRY XORN TO THE MANSION. IF I'D KNOWN THE REST OF HIS SPECIAL CLASS WAS INSIDE STARTING A RIOT, I PROBABLY WOULD HAVE HANDLED THE SITUATION DIFFERENTLY."

HELICARRIERS

S.H.I.E.L.D. HELICARRIER

ABOVE: Generations of Helicarriers relied on advanced turbo-rotor designs for lift and propulsion.
OPPOSITE: Newer Helicarrier designs combine repulsor-lift technologies with updated rotors to improve lateral maneuverability. The Statue of Liberty in the background emphasizes the Helicarrier's immense size.

DESCRIPTION AND OPERATIONAL HISTORY

The first Helicarrier was created so that S.H.I.E.L.D. Headquarters would not be based in any one of the nations that signed the treaty creating the organization. Tony Stark also backed a mobile command base on the grounds that an attack on a fixed location would provoke unwanted domestic political issues that would distract from S.H.I.E.L.D.'s main mission. When the Helicarrier was complete and the organization assembled, Nick Fury was recruited to command both.

Just as surface aircraft carriers serve as mobile command platforms and powerful force projectors, Helicarriers are a visible reminder of S.H.I.E.L.D.'s worldwide vigilance. Helicarriers are designed for a crew of more than 1,000 S.H.I.E.L.D. personnel, with facilities designed to keep the crew in the field indefinitely. In addition to living quarters and training facilities, Helicarriers come complete with multiple flight-capable escape vehicles and workshop hangars able to repair damage to any component of the vehicle or its complement of aircraft. An individual Helicarrier will typically carry S.H.I.E.L.D. proprietary vehicles such as Quinjets and flying cars, conventionally produced fighter jets, reconnaissance aircraft, and helicopters.

A Helicarrier landing deck is also long enough to accommodate full-size commercial jets. Flight-deck elevators large enough to raise a space shuttle move aircraft from the deck down to the hangar maintenance levels. *[cont. on p. 31]*

S.H.I.E.L.D.
HELICARRIER
LUXOR-CLASS, MODEL "AJAX"

COWLING TO PREVENT EXHAUST WASH FROM DAMAGING
HELICARRIER EXTERIOR OR CAUSING DANGEROUS TURBULENCE
FOR AIRCRAFT AT TAKEOFF OR LANDING

TURBINE ASSEMBLY AND EXHAUST,
PLASMA-OR REPULSOR-ASSISTED

LATERAL THRUSTERS, AIR-AND
SUBSURFACE-CAPABLE

S.H.I.E.L.D. HELICARRIER SPECS & FEATURES

LENGTH	Varies with model; typically 1,100 to 1,400 feet
WEIGHT	Varies with model; typically 100,000 to 115,000 tons
CREW CAPACITY	Approximately 1,700, independent of aircraft crew
RANGE	Unlimited
TOP SPEED	Air: 110 mph; Surface: 42 knots
POWER PLANT	Stark Resilient arc reactor; secondary/emergency power provided by tokamak fusion core
ENGINES	4 vertical turbines; 2 horizontal turbines provide aerial maneuverability and primary marine-use power
AIRCRAFT	Full complement varies; typically includes Quinjets, flying cars, military-style fighter and reconnaissance aircraft, helicopters
WEAPONRY	Turret-mounted projectile and plasma cannons; air-to-air and air-to-ground missiles; torpedoes for marine operations

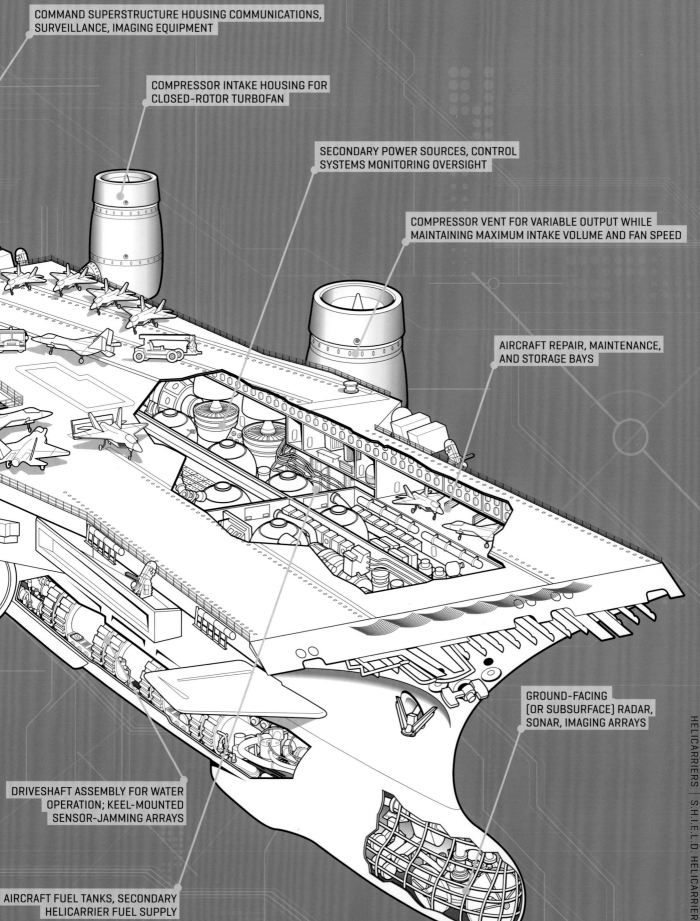

COMMAND SUPERSTRUCTURE HOUSING COMMUNICATIONS, SURVEILLANCE, IMAGING EQUIPMENT

COMPRESSOR INTAKE HOUSING FOR CLOSED-ROTOR TURBOFAN

SECONDARY POWER SOURCES, CONTROL SYSTEMS MONITORING OVERSIGHT

COMPRESSOR VENT FOR VARIABLE OUTPUT WHILE MAINTAINING MAXIMUM INTAKE VOLUME AND FAN SPEED

AIRCRAFT REPAIR, MAINTENANCE, AND STORAGE BAYS

GROUND-FACING (OR SUBSURFACE) RADAR, SONAR, IMAGING ARRAYS

DRIVESHAFT ASSEMBLY FOR WATER OPERATION; KEEL-MOUNTED SENSOR-JAMMING ARRAYS

AIRCRAFT FUEL TANKS, SECONDARY HELICARRIER FUEL SUPPLY

WHOOOM!

LEFT: One of the first Helicarriers, featuring the bridge set into the lower levels of the bow.

BELOW: The design of the Helicarrier seen to the left would become traditional but not mandatory, as seen in this model with command facilities built into the sides of the lower hull and assisted by information relayed from the flight-deck superstructure.

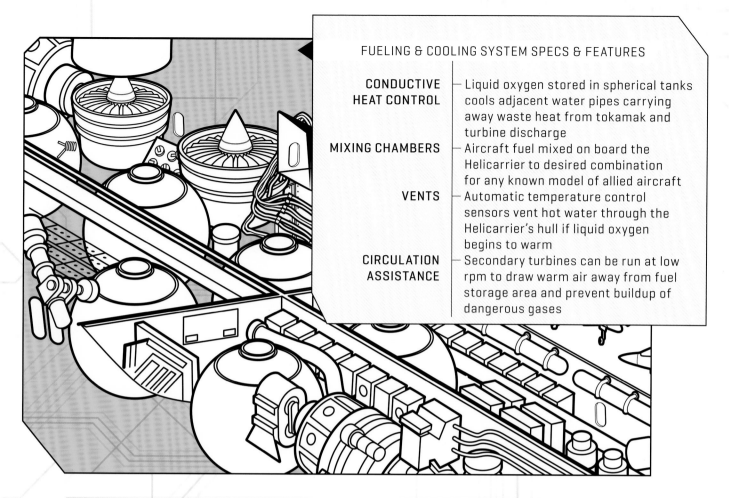

FUELING & COOLING SYSTEM SPECS & FEATURES

CONDUCTIVE HEAT CONTROL	Liquid oxygen stored in spherical tanks cools adjacent water pipes carrying away waste heat from tokamak and turbine discharge
MIXING CHAMBERS	Aircraft fuel mixed on board the Helicarrier to desired combination for any known model of allied aircraft
VENTS	Automatic temperature control sensors vent hot water through the Helicarrier's hull if liquid oxygen begins to warm
CIRCULATION ASSISTANCE	Secondary turbines can be run at low rpm to draw warm air away from fuel storage area and prevent buildup of dangerous gases

In general, Helicarriers are noted for their huge internal spaces, dedicated to repair and maintenance of S.H.I.E.L.D. fleets.

The operational range of Helicarriers has always been unlimited. Early models were nuclear powered, while more recent versions have incorporated Stark Industries innovations in repulsor and vortex-beam technology, powered by advanced tokamak-style fusion cores.

The Helicarrier bridge, generally a multifloor space, set in the lower floors of the forward portion of the hull below the flight deck, is a comprehensive command center with feeds from every satellite network on Earth. Intelligence officers maintain continuous surveillance of electronic communications worldwide, with a particular focus on current mission priorities. Piggybacking on government surveillance networks, Helicarrier personnel are able to access real-time aerial and ground-level views of every city on Earth and many places in between. Due to Tony Stark's influential position within S.H.I.E.L.D., the Helicarrier also has access to Stark technologies. The advanced research of Wakanda Design Group is also part of Helicarrier command systems.

Early Helicarriers flew using enormous rotors made of advanced alloys capable of withstanding the astronomical torque required to generate enough lift to keep a vehicle of such size in the air. Other closed rotors and a multidirection system of thrust deflectors provided horizontal control. As energy thruster technologies evolved, they were incorporated into Helicarriers on a massive scale, using a

TURBINE SPECS & FEATURES

LENGTH	231 feet, 8 inches including exhaust nozzle
DIAMETER	76 feet, 9 inches at widest point near hull mount
MAXIMUM RPM	22,000
THRUST	64 million pounds at maximum intake
TURBINE BLADES	Manufactured from S.H.I.E.L.D.-proprietary ceramic/metallic alloy to withstand torque of rotational velocity with blade length of 32 feet

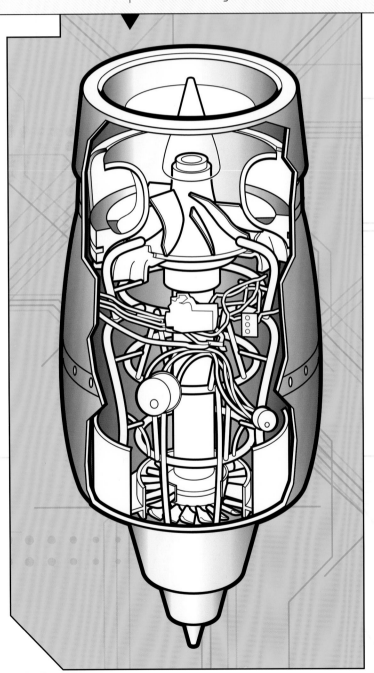

combination of rotor lift and keel-mounted thrusters to achieve increased agility, range, and stability.

Newer generations of the Helicarrier have made use of advanced vortex beam technology to provide more thrust and maneuverability in a much smaller and more efficient engine assembly. Their power plants are also newer, incorporating new advances in fusion technology. Lighter than previous reactors, these new plants have a much higher yield, permitting the full application of vortex beam technology, which had previously been available only in smaller vehicles.

WEAPONRY

Helicarrier weapons systems have evolved over time. Classes of weapon common to all Helicarriers are air-to-air missiles, rapid-fire 20mm and 40mm cannons, particle-beam turrets, and batteries of cruise missiles. Under a special dispensation to anti-proliferation treaties, they also carry nuclear missiles.

Helicarriers are heavily armored and outfitted with electronic and conventional antimissile defense systems. What they lack in maneuverability they make up for in durability. Newer models feature antipsionic shielding for command-and-control systems, for protection against telepathic or psychokinetic attacks. Further counterintelligence measures include a stasis field enveloping the Helicarrier. All computer chips and drives removed from this field immediately dump their data and self-destruct, preventing hostile forces from capturing vital records and files.

Several Helicarriers have been destroyed despite these features, underscoring the lethal nature of the threats S.H.I.E.L.D. faces.

ABOVE: More recent generations of the Helicarrier feature rotor assemblies that can be rotated for directional thrust. In this case, even full rotation could not prevent a loss of lift.

NICK FURY

"PEOPLE SEE THE HELICARRIER AS THE HEART AND SOUL OF S.H.I.E.L.D. THAT'S GOOD. THAT'S WHAT I WANT THEM TO SEE. BECAUSE THAT MEANS I HAVE A LITTLE SECRET: THE HEART AND SOUL OF S.H.I.E.L.D. ARE ITS AGENTS, FROM THE MECHANICS TURNING WRENCHES DOWN IN THE HANGARS ALL THE WAY UP TO STARK AND ROGERS. DON'T GET ME WRONG, THOUGH. IT'S A LOT EASIER TO RELY ON YOUR PEOPLE WHEN THEY'RE BACKED UP BY THE MOST POWERFUL COMBAT VESSEL THE WORLD HAS EVER SEEN."

MONSTER HUNTING HELICARRIER

Nick Fury's associate Dum Dum Dugan commanded a Helicarrier purpose-built to capture and hold the gargantuan monsters collectively known as kaiju. This Helicarrier was outfitted with nets designed to restrain a creature hundreds of feet tall, high-energy stun beams, gas-launched cables to entangle the kaiju's limbs, and a complete research laboratory intended for the study and analysis of the monster once it was captured. An early prototype of this Helicarrier did not survive its initial kaiju encounter, but the full-size version completed the mission.

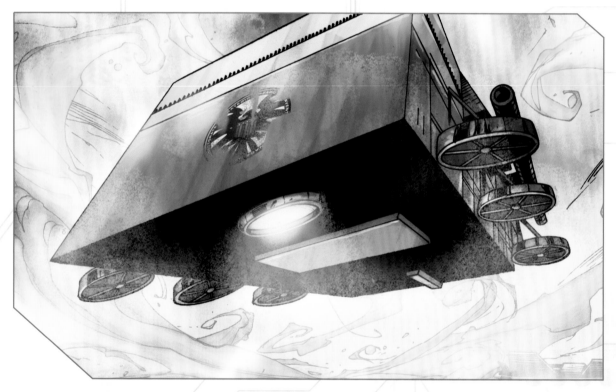

MONSTER HUNTING HELICARRIER SPECS & FEATURES

FACILITIES	Xenobiology research labs replacing space dedicated to aircraft operations in a standard Helicarrier
ARMAMENTS	Ordnance package designed for (primarily nonlethal) high impact on kaiju-size creatures, including missiles, flash and stun beams, sonic projectors; tools for capture and restraint include cables, nets, and sedatives tailored to the genome of specific targets (where available)

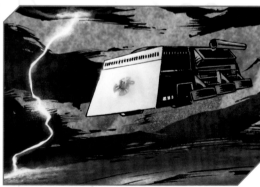

TOP & ABOVE: The Monster Hunting Helicarrier design reflects its unique mission. Its hull has a large central space for holding captured kaiju, while the retractable hatch on the bottom of the craft allows for intake of subdued creatures as the vehicle remains airborne.

ILIAD

ILIAD SPECS & FEATURES

- **CREW CAPACITY** 4,400; operational minimum 62
- **PROPULSION** 4 vortex-beam projectors powered by Stark Industries arc reactors
- **HULL** Stealth materials bonded to armor plating 32 inches thick
- **INSTRUMENTS** Electronic and psionic jamming arrays; full-spectrum audiovisual surveillance with an effective range to the horizon; encrypted taps on satellite networks
- **OPERATIONAL LIMITS** Not designed for marine use; airborne only

ABOVE: The Iliad maintains the standard Helicarrier features of a forward-facing launch bay and lower-deck bridge. Repulsor-based propulsion has completely replaced rotor lift, and the overall look is a throwback to riveted World War II—era designs—which isn't a surprise, since Iliad was designed under the direction of Steve Rogers.

Following the resurgence of H.A.M.M.E.R., Steve Rogers commissioned a new Helicarrier and made it the mobile headquarters of the Secret Avengers, with Maria Hill as ship commander. Iliad, as it came to be known, is the most advanced Helicarrier yet. One departure from previous generations of Helicarriers is that Iliad has an entire operational center dedicated to psychological, telepathic, and psionic attacks. Agents and assets in the Psy Ops Center have their psionic abilities intensified by a neuropathic matrix and a series of signal boosters. With a powerful telepath at the center of the matrix, Iliad is effectively an Omega-level psionic weapon.

H.A.M.M.E.R. HELICARRIER

ABOVE: The H.A.M.M.E.R. Helicarrier's design recalls a dreadnought battleship rather than a flat-topped aircraft carrier.

OPPOSITE TOP: Bristling with visible armaments rather than a flight deck and hangar bays, the H.A.M.M.E.R. Helicarrier conveyed a very different impression than its S.H.I.E.L.D. predecessor.

OPPOSITE BOTTOM: The H.A.M.M.E.R. Helicarrier was a visible show of strength in the skies over Oklahoma during the siege of Asgard.

DESCRIPTION AND OPERATIONAL HISTORY

When Norman Osborn dismantled S.H.I.E.L.D. and created H.A.M.M.E.R., he also decommissioned existing Helicarriers in favor of a new design. H.A.M.M.E.R. Helicarriers didn't have a flight deck, and their propulsion systems differed from the keel-mounted thrusters and lateral vortex engines that S.H.I.E.L.D. used in recent Helicarrier generations. They featured heavy cannons mounted at the base of their wings and lighter armaments at a number of other reinforced hardpoints on the armored exterior. S.H.I.E.L.D. Helicarriers were intended primarily as mobile command posts, with fleets of light aircraft for strike capability. H.A.M.M.E.R. Helicarriers were heavy assault vehicles, with a secondary function as command and control. Essentially they were flight-capable battleships, designed to instill fear.

Most of what is known about the H.A.M.M.E.R. Helicarriers comes from Black Widow and Bucky Barnes, who infiltrated Osborn's command vessel in search of information regarding the whereabouts of Steve Rogers. Osborn's records suggest more than one of the vehicles was constructed. Other than the one destroyed during the siege of Asgard, the fate of these Helicarriers is not presently known.

CYCLOPS

"OSBORN KNEW A GOOD THING WHEN HE SAW IT, AND ONE OF THE FIRST THINGS HE DID AS HEAD OF H.A.M.M.E.R. WAS COMMISSION HELICARRIERS, H.A.M.M.E.R.-STYLE. UGLY THINGS, ALL POINTS AND CANNON BARRELS. HE WANTED IT UGLY, TOO, BECAUSE THAT WAY IT WOULD SCARE PEOPLE. STARK HAD THE RIGHT IDEA. HE COMMANDEERED THAT BEAST AFTER THE U.S. ARMY AND AIR FORCE LIT IT UP, AND WENT KAMIKAZE ON THE VOID. BEST THING THAT COULD HAVE HAPPENED TO IT, IF YOU ASK ME. DON'T THINK I'VE EVEN BEEN SO HAPPY TO SEE A BILLION DOLLARS' WORTH OF ADVANCED MILITARY HARDWARE GO UP IN FLAMES."

H.A.M.M.E.R. HELICARRIER
OS/T ALPHA MK 1

WING-MOUNTED PLASMA CANNON FLANKED BY RAPID-FIRE ENERGY CANNON BATTERIES

AUTOMATED FIRE-CONTROL RECEPTOR IDENTIFIES AND DESTROYS INCOMING VEHICLES AND MISSILES

ENHANCED ARMOR PLATING OVER BRIDGE AND OTHER CRITICAL AREAS

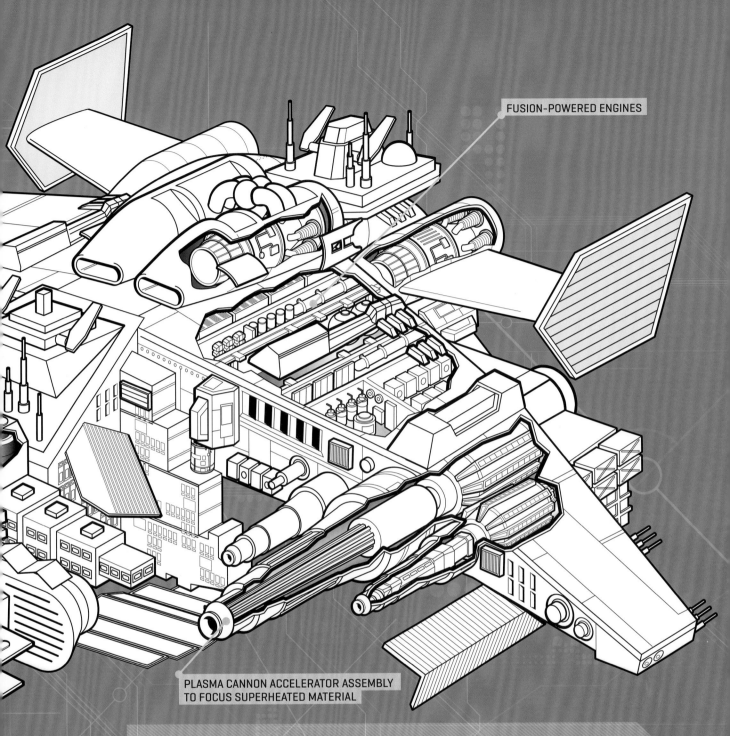

FUSION-POWERED ENGINES

PLASMA CANNON ACCELERATOR ASSEMBLY
TO FOCUS SUPERHEATED MATERIAL

H.A.M.M.E.R. HELICARRIER SPECS & FEATURES

LENGTH	948 feet, 11 inches
WEIGHT	75,000 tons
CREW CAPACITY	240; additional capacity of 1,000 H.A.M.M.E.R. soldiers
AIRCRAFT	Full complement of 84 H.A.M.M.E.R. Sky-Cycles
POWER PLANT	Oscorp ZV-88i fusion reactors
ENGINES	Oscorp KO-225 particle thrusters
RANGE	Unlimited
WEAPONRY	Twin batteries of fixed plasma and energy cannons; nose-mounted missile tubes and EMP projector

ABOVE: Surrounded by squadrons of the
H.A.M.M.E.R. version of the Sky-Cycle
and led by the formidable Dark Avengers,
the H.A.M.M.E.R. Helicarrier was an
intimidating sight indeed.

RIGHT: The heavily armored and shielded
H.A.M.M.E.R. Helicarrier is untroubled
by lightning strikes or emanations of
mystical energy.

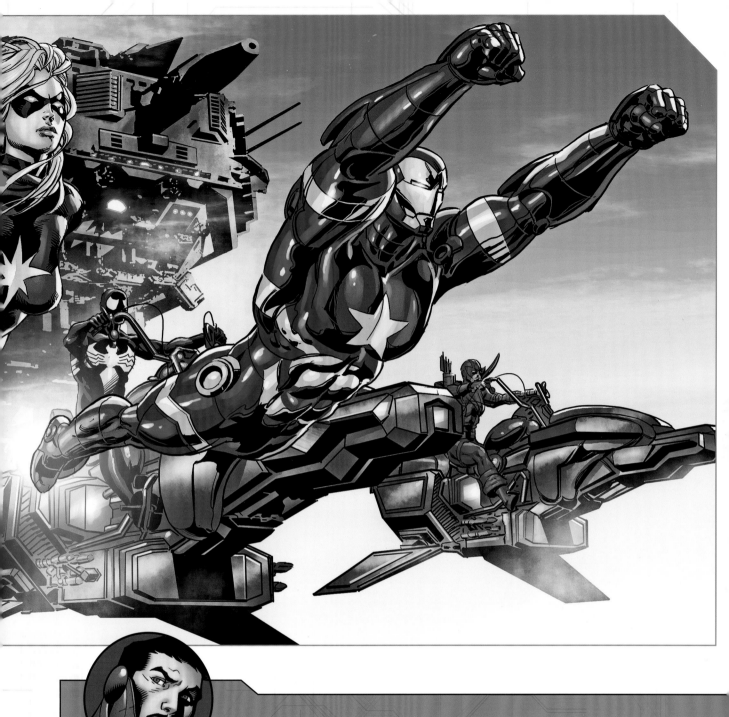

TONY STARK

"BAD SITUATION. AFTER BULLSEYE KILLED HIS WIFE, THE SENTRY—A.K.A. ROBERT REYNOLDS—WENT NUTS AND TURNED INTO THE VOID. TENTACLES IN THE SKY, THE WHOLE WORKS, WHICH WAS JUST WHAT OSBORN WANTED AT FIRST, BUT THEN HE FOUND OUT WHAT THE REST OF US ALREADY KNEW: YOU JUST DON'T EVER WANT THE VOID AROUND. BY THE TIME I GOT CONTROL OF OSBORN'S HELICARRIER, THE VOID HAD ALREADY KILLED ARES AND DESTROYED MOST OF ASGARD. HE WAS ABOUT TO DO THOR IN. I COULDN'T FACE HIM HEAD-ON. NONE OF US COULD. THE ONLY THING I COULD THINK OF WAS TO PLASTER HIM WITH THE BIGGEST, HEAVIEST THING AROUND . . . AND IT TURNED OUT THAT A DAMAGED H.A.M.M.E.R. HELICARRIER WAS JUST THE THING. I'M JUST GLAD I GOT OUT BEFORE IT BLEW UP. THEN I WAS GLAD I GOT OUT OF THE WAY WHEN THOR GOT UP AND BROUGHT THE LIGHTNING TO FINISH THE VOID OFF. IT WAS KIND OF TOO BAD. ROBBIE WAS A DECENT GUY BEFORE COSMIC POWERS WENT TO HIS HEAD."

DEPARTMENT H HELICARRIER

DEPARTMENT H HELICARRIER SPECS & FEATURES

LENGTH	759 feet
WEIGHT	42,000 tons
CREW CAPACITY	116, independent of deployable Department H combat personnel
AIRCRAFT	Omnijet; several military-comparable fighter aircraft and combat helicopters
POWER PLANT	Fusion reactor, secondary power systems run by plasma reservoir
PROPULSION	Variable-inlet ramjets mounted under the base of each wing, each producing in excess of forty million pounds of lift; twin repulsor-powered engines mounted on the bottom of the hull provide flight stability and additional lift
ARMAMENTS	Rear turret-mounted plasma cannons; air-to-air missile batteries; wing-mounted 18mm Gatling cannons; electronic countermeasures including narrowband EMP

ABOVE: The Department H Helicarrier was designed as a mobile base for the Canadian team Omega Flight. Without S.H.I.E.L.D.'s international reach and mandate, there was no need to include full hangar bays and support for worldwide deployments.

OPPOSITE: The difference in size between the Department H Helicarrier and its S.H.I.E.L.D. counterpart is clear in this image, captured near an Origin Bomb detonation in Canada.

TONY STARK

"DEPARTMENT H SAW WHAT S.H.I.E.L.D. WAS DOING AND DECIDED THEY NEEDED THEIR OWN HELICARRIER. PART OF THE IDEA WAS THAT THEIR NEW GUYS, OMEGA FLIGHT, WOULD BE THEIR VERSION OF THE AVENGERS. EVERYBODY WANTS AVENGERS. ONLY PROBLEM WITH THAT PLAN WAS THAT MOST OF THE TEAM DIDN'T MAKE IT THROUGH ONE OF THEIR FIRST DEPLOYMENTS. THEY WENT TO CHECK OUT THE SITE OF AN ORIGIN BOMB IN SASKATCHEWAN. THEN THEY ALL DISAPPEARED, SEALED INSIDE A WEIRD SPOOKY SPHERE. IT TOOK REAL AVENGERS TO GET TO THEM ...HER, I SHOULD SAY. VALIDATOR WAS ONE OF THE NEW KIDS IN DEPARTMENT H, AND SHE WAS ALSO THE ONLY SURVIVOR OF WHATEVER HAPPENED AT THE SITE OF THE ORIGIN BOMB. I'D NEVER MET HER BEFORE AND I COULD TELL THAT AFTER BEING IN PROXIMITY TO THE BOMB SHE WAS ...DIFFERENT. YOU WANT TO KNOW MORE, LOOK IT UP. FREAKS ME OUT JUST REMEMBERING IT.

WE DECIDED TO SHARE TECHNOLOGY WITH DEPARTMENT H BECAUSE THEY NEEDED A WAY TO GET THEIR GUYS AROUND FAST, AND WITH LOTS OF TECH AND FIRE SUPPORT. CANADA'S BIG. THE DEPARTMENT H HELICARRIER DOESN'T HAVE A FLIGHT DECK LIKE THE S.H.I.E.L.D. VERSIONS, BECAUSE DEPARTMENT H DOESN'T HAVE ENOUGH JETS TO NEED ONE. ALSO THEIR HELICARRIER IS A LOT MORE MOBILE; ONE THING ABOUT S.H.I.E.L.D. HELICARRIERS IS THEY STEER LIKE DEAD PIGS. THE CANUCK VERSION KIND OF REMINDS ME OF ONE OF THE MINI-HELICARRIERS WRECKED WAY BACK IN ONE OF THE GIANT-MONSTER BATTLES. I LIKE WHAT THEY DID OVERALL. NOT AS GOOD AS SOMETHING I'D BUILD, BUT I JUST MIGHT BORROW A DESIGN ELEMENT OR TWO FROM THIS MODEL WHEN I WORK ON THE NEXT GENERATION OF HELICARRIERS FOR FURY."

AIRCRAFT

AVENGERS QUINJET

ABOVE: The frequency of Quinjet crashes has an upside: It allows for frequent updates on the original designs, with improvements each time.

OPPOSITE TOP: Quinjets come especially in handy in places like the Savage Land, where the local fauna make quick work of less maneuverable craft.

OPPOSITE BOTTOM: Compact size and VTOL capability make the Quinjet a perfect vehicle for small-group operations in crowded environments, such as urban parklands

DESCRIPTION AND OPERATIONAL HISTORY

Created by Wakanda Design Group, with Black Panther leading the design team, the Quinjet has been the Avengers' preferred method of small-group transportation for decades. The original Quinjets could carry seven people and reach a speed of Mach 2.1, propelled by two banks of dual turbojet engines, with a fifth engine primarily used for directional thrust and VTOL capability via a forward-facing thrust deflector. The Quinjet's climbing speed of 7,900 feet per minute and operational range of 9,500 miles quickly made it indispensable to the Avengers' expansive mission needs. Later models would incorporate advanced repulsor-based thrusters, positioned along the sides and bottom of the fuselage, to achieve more efficient VTOL performance, but the five-engine design quickly became the favored configuration and has rarely been altered.

Although fast and reliable, Quinjets are lightly armored and unarmed. Their service lives are often very short, a precedent established on Black Panther's shakedown flight of the very first model. *[cont. on p. 51]*

QUINJET
1960S-ERA "CLASSIC"

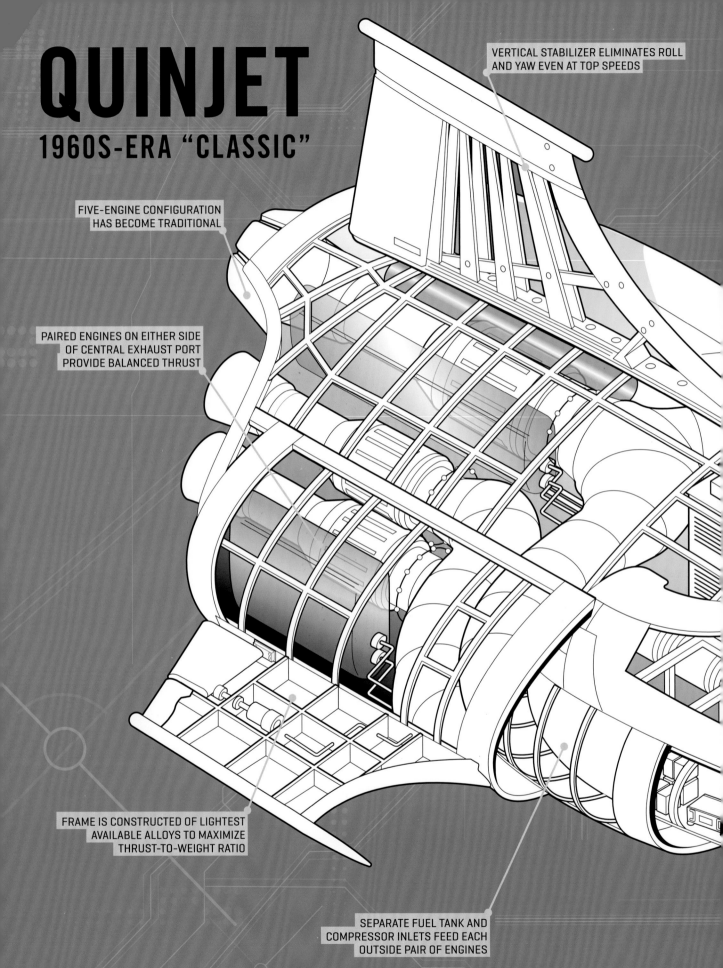

VERTICAL STABILIZER ELIMINATES ROLL AND YAW EVEN AT TOP SPEEDS

FIVE-ENGINE CONFIGURATION HAS BECOME TRADITIONAL

PAIRED ENGINES ON EITHER SIDE OF CENTRAL EXHAUST PORT PROVIDE BALANCED THRUST

FRAME IS CONSTRUCTED OF LIGHTEST AVAILABLE ALLOYS TO MAXIMIZE THRUST-TO-WEIGHT RATIO

SEPARATE FUEL TANK AND COMPRESSOR INLETS FEED EACH OUTSIDE PAIR OF ENGINES

CLASSIC QUINJET SPECS & FEATURES

CREW CAPACITY	4 standard; some variations carry more
WEAPONRY	None
ENGINES	Five hot-inlet turbojets with separate intakes, based on Stark Industries designs
MAX SPEED	Mach 2.1
RANGE	10,000 miles
ALTITUDE CEILING	117,000 feet
INSTRUMENTATION	Autopilot capable of executing VTOL; infrared-to-ultraviolet scanning; radio intercept package; encrypted narrowcast to dedicated receiver at Avengers Mansion

TWIN FUSELAGE AIR INTAKES JOIN AT A SINGLE COMPRESSOR

WINGS ARE EQUIPPED WITH SENSOR ARRAYS AND ELECTRONIC COUNTERMEASURE SUITES

COCKPIT COMMUNICATIONS AND MONITORING EQUIPMENT

STEERING YOKES AUTOMATICALLY DEFER PRIORITY IF ONE IS DAMAGED

STORAGE CAPACITY BETWEEN INTERIOR BULK HEAD AND HULL CARRIES SCIENTIFIC EQUIPMENT AND SURVIVAL SUPPLIES

TOP: This Quinjet got a little too close to a titanic battle in the Savage Land.
ABOVE: The first generation of spaceflight-capable Quinjets were designed with heavier hulls and increased thruster power to achieve escape velocity and survive the rigors of atmospheric reentry.

Despite their lack of armament, Quinjets are not without defensive measures. Each is equipped with electronic countermeasures, including signal jamming and anti-targeting systems. Onboard instrumentation includes cameras, multispectral surveillance arrays, and phased array radar designed to bypass stealth technologies.

The Quinjet's nimble controls and small size make it a difficult target. The craft's lack of weaponry is a deliberate choice on the part of Wakanda Design Group and the Avengers, reflecting a desire to avoid a militaristic public image.

SPACE-CAPABLE QUINJETS

Wakanda Design Group has continued to refine the Quinjet design, and so has Tony Stark. From the beginning, Quinjets were designed for high-altitude capability. Early models had flight ceilings of 130,000 feet, well into Earth's stratosphere. With afterburners, this could be extended briefly as high as 220,000 feet, midway through the mesosphere. Cabin insulation protects passengers and crew from temperatures as high as 130 degrees Fahrenheit. Specialized larger versions, with upgraded life-support systems and engines designed to perform in complete vacuum, have been created for space travel and used as rapid small-group transports for near-Earth missions, as in one battle against an interstellar alien alliance controlled by Thanos.

ABOVE: Quinjets are housed in dedicated hangars such as the one seen here, set below ground level adjacent to Avengers Tower. The hangar roof retracts for takeoff and landing, and an underground passage connects to the lower levels of Avengers Tower.

The smaller wing area reflects the lack of lift available in space, although the wings are still large enough to stabilize the craft in atmospheric flight. Space-capable Quinjets also carry deep space survival gear customized to the individual needs of each team member.

NEWEST GENERATIONS

Innovations on display in newer generations of Quinjets include multidirectional thrusters spaced along either side of the fuselage. This propulsion arrangement increases maneuverability and low-speed VTOL control in tight spaces. These Quinjets are larger than previous generations, reflecting their dual-purpose design suited for both atmospheric and near-Earth space operation. The larger size allows for a bi-level cockpit and common area, dividing crew and passengers. The red tinting of this model's windows is an aesthetic choice by Tony Stark and has no functional purpose.

The most recent generation of Quinjets has added aquatic operation to its mission capabilities. Advances in propulsion technology have permitted new thrusters that do not require oxygen intake. Also, since they use energy field–contained plasma conduits instead of open nozzles, there is no issue with water entering the exhaust ports. Exit portals are also sealed by force fields, permitting crew members to exit underwater without breaching the integrity of the cabin or life-support systems. Antenna arrays and other equipment that may be damaged

BELOW: Directional thrusters on the lateral edges of the fuselage and below the passenger compartment provide precise flight control and nimble aerial performance—both necessary for an unarmed transport vehicle.

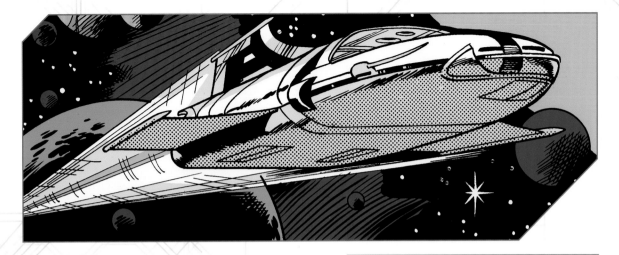

by underwater operation retract into fuselage housings for subsurface operation. Quinjets are still designed primarily for atmospheric use and are not rated for depths below 100 meters.

INFINITY CRUSADE

Tony Stark adapted the Quinjet technology and chassis to create a larger, fully interstellar-capable craft to be used in the Avengers' attempts to prevent Thanos from assembling the Infinity Gauntlet. These vehicles were rounder in profile and coated with reflective material to disperse the heat of re-entry. Shielding built into the hull protected the crew from the radiation of interstellar space. As with the earlier generation of Quinjets designed for near-Earth use, these had smaller wings than those created primarily for atmospheric deployment, with steering reassigned to a number of angled secondary thrusters set along the underside of the hull. The craft's larger size allowed for full life-support systems including oxygen recapture, and large supplies of food and water for trips of uncertain duration.

TOP: This version of the Quinjet is engineered for deep space operation. Note the reflective hull, smaller windows, and shorter wings.

ABOVE LEFT: Stealth modes derived from the Dagger Quinjet make it easier for Quinjets to operate in and around large cities without drawing civilian attention.

TONY STARK

THE INFINITY CRUSADE WASN'T THE FIRST TIME A QUINJET HAD GONE FASTER THAN THE SPEED OF LIGHT. YEARS BEFORE, THOR MODIFIED ONE ON THE FLY FOR FASTER-THAN-LIGHT TRAVEL, IN THIS CASE BY MEANS OF HIS HAMMER MJOLNIR. I'M NOT GOING TO SAY THOR GAVE ME THE IDEA, EXACTLY, BUT IT DID FOCUS MY THINKING ON HOW I MIGHT BE ABLE TO SURMOUNT THE OLD E=MC² PROBLEM. GOOD THING I FINALLY FIGURED IT OUT WHEN I DID.

QUINJET 2
MODEL ST-2011

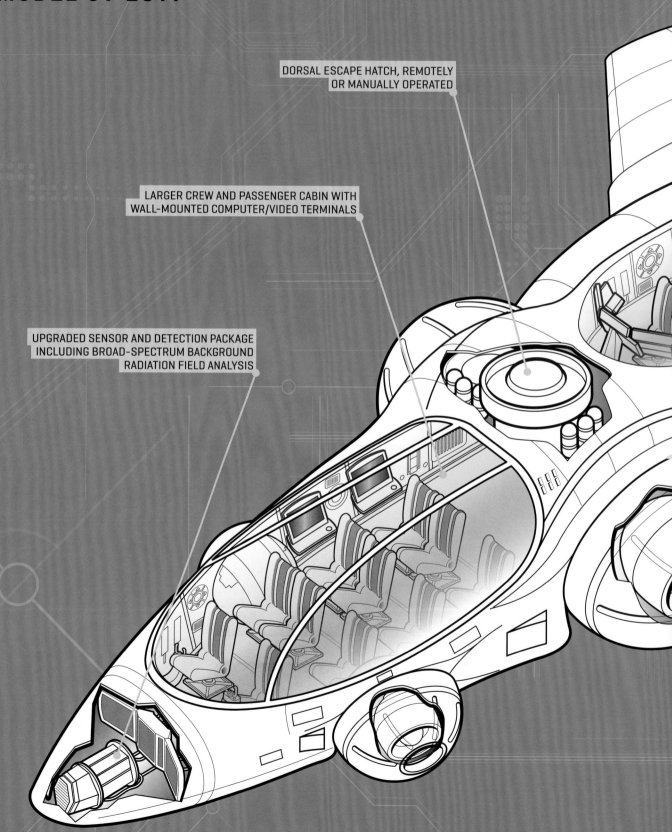

DORSAL ESCAPE HATCH, REMOTELY OR MANUALLY OPERATED

LARGER CREW AND PASSENGER CABIN WITH WALL-MOUNTED COMPUTER/VIDEO TERMINALS

UPGRADED SENSOR AND DETECTION PACKAGE INCLUDING BROAD-SPECTRUM BACKGROUND RADIATION FIELD ANALYSIS

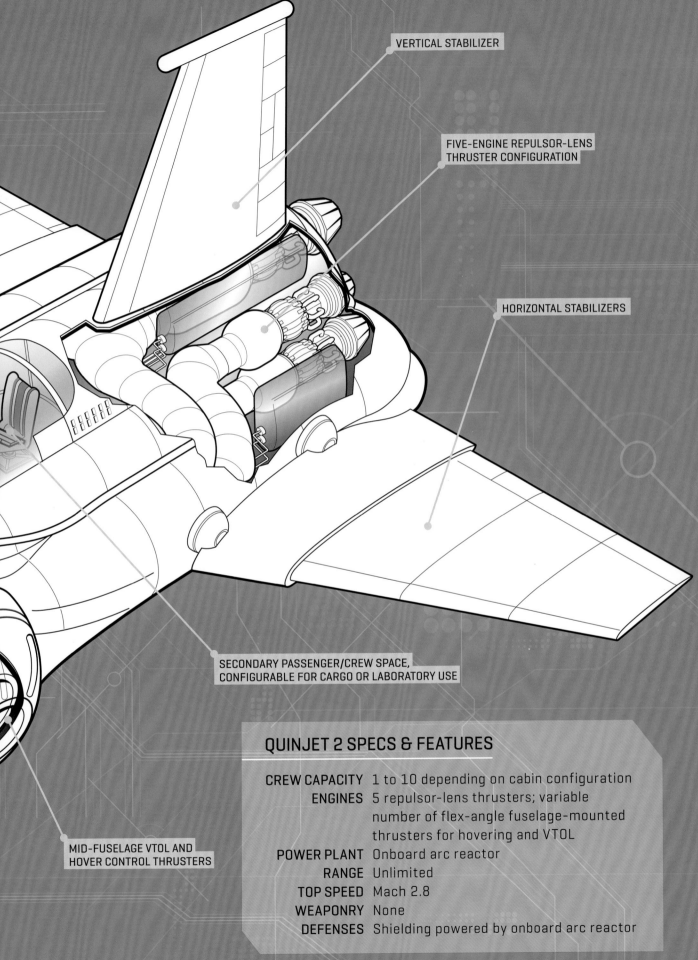

VERTICAL STABILIZER

FIVE-ENGINE REPULSOR-LENS
THRUSTER CONFIGURATION

HORIZONTAL STABILIZERS

SECONDARY PASSENGER/CREW SPACE,
CONFIGURABLE FOR CARGO OR LABORATORY USE

MID-FUSELAGE VTOL AND
HOVER CONTROL THRUSTERS

QUINJET 2 SPECS & FEATURES

CREW CAPACITY	1 to 10 depending on cabin configuration
ENGINES	5 repulsor-lens thrusters; variable number of flex-angle fuselage-mounted thrusters for hovering and VTOL
POWER PLANT	Onboard arc reactor
RANGE	Unlimited
TOP SPEED	Mach 2.8
WEAPONRY	None
DEFENSES	Shielding powered by onboard arc reactor

DAGGER QUINJET

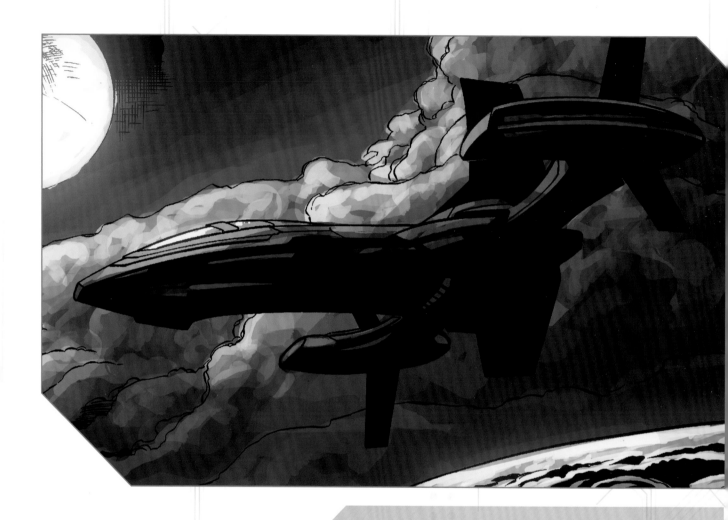

DAGGER QUINJET
SPECS & FEATURES

- **CREW CAPACITY** 8
- **PROPULSION** Twin Wakanda Design Group particle engines, with exhaust baffles to decrease heat signature
- **MAX SPEED** Mach 1
- **MAX ALTITUDE** 71,000 feet
- **FEATURES** Vibranium-threaded hull design scrambles radar signature; multiple vertical stabilizers provide very low stall speed before VTOL directional thrusters must be engaged

When Doctor Doom took control of Wakanda's supply of Vibranium, Black Panther's personal commando team known as the Midnight Angels were sent on a strike mission into Latveria. For this mission, they used a stealth-modified Quinjet known as the Dagger. The Dagger's fuselage material was a radar-absorbent composite of Vibranium alloys and ceramics, making it lighter than normal aircraft of comparable size and also invisible to most detection systems. The craft also featured electronic countermeasures that analyzed incoming radar signals and emitted electronic noise designed to baffle the specific radar frequency being used. It was matte black to decrease its visual profile, and its recessed thruster housings cut down on visible exhaust. Thermal detection of the Dagger was also difficult due to its low-temperature ion propulsion systems.

THUNDERBOLTS QUINJET

Oscorp created its own Quinjet variant for the H.A.M.M.E.R. strike team known as the Thunderbolts, departing from the traditional design for a more menacing look. These jets were larger and faster than the Avengers' Quinjets, with updated armor materials and increased carrying capacity. Batwing flourishes to the design and black coloration distinguished these vehicles from Avengers Quinjets. Few were built, and none remain in service.

THUNDERBOLTS QUINJET SPECS & FEATURES

CREW CAPACITY	Maximum 20
PROPULSION	Repulsor-lens thrusters derived from Stark Industries models
RANGE	Unlimited
MAX SPEED	Mach 3.3
MAX ALTITUDE	66,000 feet
FEATURES	Advanced composite alloy hull exterior diminishes radar profile and provides improved protection against energy and kinetic impacts

OPPOSITE: The Dagger featured more wing surface area, widely spaced thrust points, and multiple vertical steering planes, critical for operation at the lower airspeeds required for effective stealth operation.
BELOW: Thunderbolts Quinjets adopted a bird-of-prey design to instill fear in enemies.

S.H.I.E.L.D. FLYING CAR

DESCRIPTION AND OPERATIONAL HISTORY

Created by Stark Industries for S.H.I.E.L.D., flying cars have become the most recognizable S.H.I.E.L.D. asset other than the Helicarrier. Most are based on high-performance sports cars, reflecting Stark's love of both speed and style. For S.H.I.E.L.D. use, cars are given upgraded powertrains, steering, and suspension. Windows and doors are armored with internal composite layers.

The signature technology of the flying car is, of course, its ability to levitate. The car's wheels are actually highly advanced, multifunctional assemblies, delivering high-performance steering and suspension. At the touch of a button on the steering column, however, the wheels rotate into a position parallel with the ground and rockets housed in each wheel activate. The technology of these rockets has advanced over time. Different models have used high-speed mini-turbines, ion-repelling thrusters, repulsor lenses based on Tony Stark's Iron Man suit technology, and miniaturized versions of the vortex-beam technology now standard on Helicarriers. The car's maximum airspeed is typically somewhere near Mach 1.

BELOW: A flying car and allied helicopter. Note the newest generation of wheel-mounted repulsor-lift engines.
OPPOSITE: Deadpool has stolen . . . um, borrowed . . . just about every other kind of vehicle. Why not a candy-apple-red flying car, too?

ABOVE: Captain America in a recent flying car model. Note the more compact rotating wheel assemblies.

OPPOSITE TOP: Flying cars have been adapted for use in just about any potential operational environment. Here, rocket-style thrusters enable controlled spaceflight.

OPPOSITE BOTTOM: Nick Fury and his Howling Commandos comrade Dum Dum Dugan take a ride in one of the early flying cars.

In order to power a car's flight capability, its engine has to be upgraded beyond the standard internal combustion model. The first flying cars used compact 350-horsepower turbines for ground power, with a thrust deflector designed to lift the front wheels when the driver triggered the flight mechanism. This enabled the front wheels to rotate into position and provide initial vertical thrust to get the car off the ground, at which time the rear wheels would rotate into their flight configuration and activate. In current models the turbine engine has been superseded by miniaturized arc reactor technologies.

Flying cars have a variety of onboard weapons systems. Trunk-mounted missiles are standard equipment, and the Mark V, standard for many years, also deployed a 20mm cannon from the front grille and a 30mm cannon turret from the rear, housed next to the missile launcher. Defensive measures for aerial use include anti-missile chaff. The driver's seat can eject by means of explosive bolts and includes a parachute that deploys from the back of the seat.

More recently, flying cars have also been built without weapons systems. The reduction in weight enables longer service range and greater speed, as well as increased passenger capacity. *[cont. on p. 65]*

FIRST FLYING CAR SPECS & FEATURES

CREW CAPACITY	2
ENGINE	350-horsepower turbine engine under hood for ground operation. Exhaust fed through 4 variable-angle high-speed rotors in wheel assemblies for aerial operations
MAX ALTITUDE	10,000 feet
MAX SPEED	Mach 1
WEAPONRY	Trunk-mounted anti-aircraft missiles

S.H.I.E.L.D. FLYING CAR

MODEL SFC-13-G

FLYING CAR SPECS & FEATURES

CREW CAPACITY	2
ENGINES	High-compression turbine engine under hood for ground operation; 4 independently variable lift generators (turbine or repulsor-lift) in wheel assemblies for aerial operations
MAX ALTITUDE	17,000 feet
MAX SPEED	Mach 1.2
WEAPONRY	Auto-targeting 20mm Gatling turrets, hood- and trunk-mounted; rear turret also includes air-to-air missile battery
DEFENSIVE MEASURES	Anti-radar chaff; radar and visual surveillance jamming

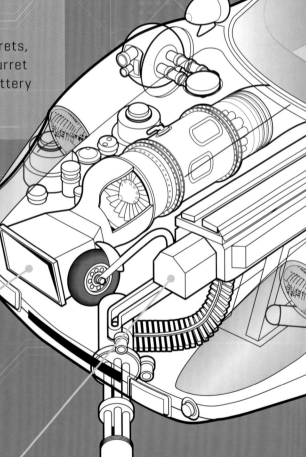

PASSENGER SEAT SEPARATELY EJECTABLE IF CAR'S FLIGHT CAPABILITY IS COMPROMISED

INTAKE FOR TURBINE ENGINE

HOUSING FOR BELT-FED, FRONT-MOUNTED 20MM GATLING CANNON

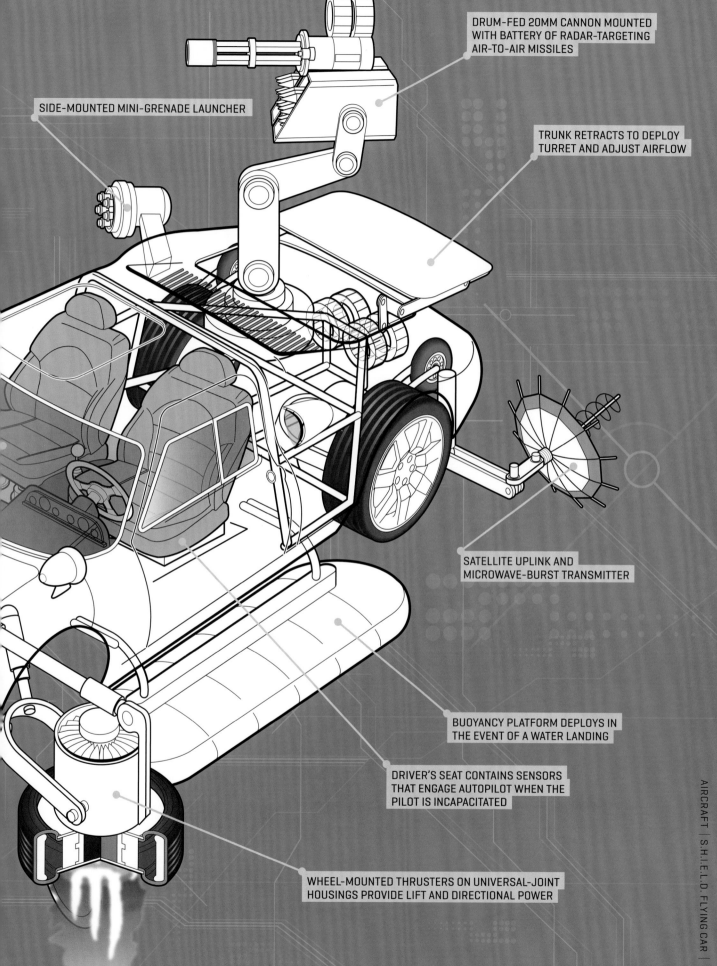

DRUM-FED 20MM CANNON MOUNTED WITH BATTERY OF RADAR-TARGETING AIR-TO-AIR MISSILES

SIDE-MOUNTED MINI-GRENADE LAUNCHER

TRUNK RETRACTS TO DEPLOY TURRET AND ADJUST AIRFLOW

SATELLITE UPLINK AND MICROWAVE-BURST TRANSMITTER

BUOYANCY PLATFORM DEPLOYS IN THE EVENT OF A WATER LANDING

DRIVER'S SEAT CONTAINS SENSORS THAT ENGAGE AUTOPILOT WHEN THE PILOT IS INCAPACITATED

WHEEL-MOUNTED THRUSTERS ON UNIVERSAL-JOINT HOUSINGS PROVIDE LIFT AND DIRECTIONAL POWER

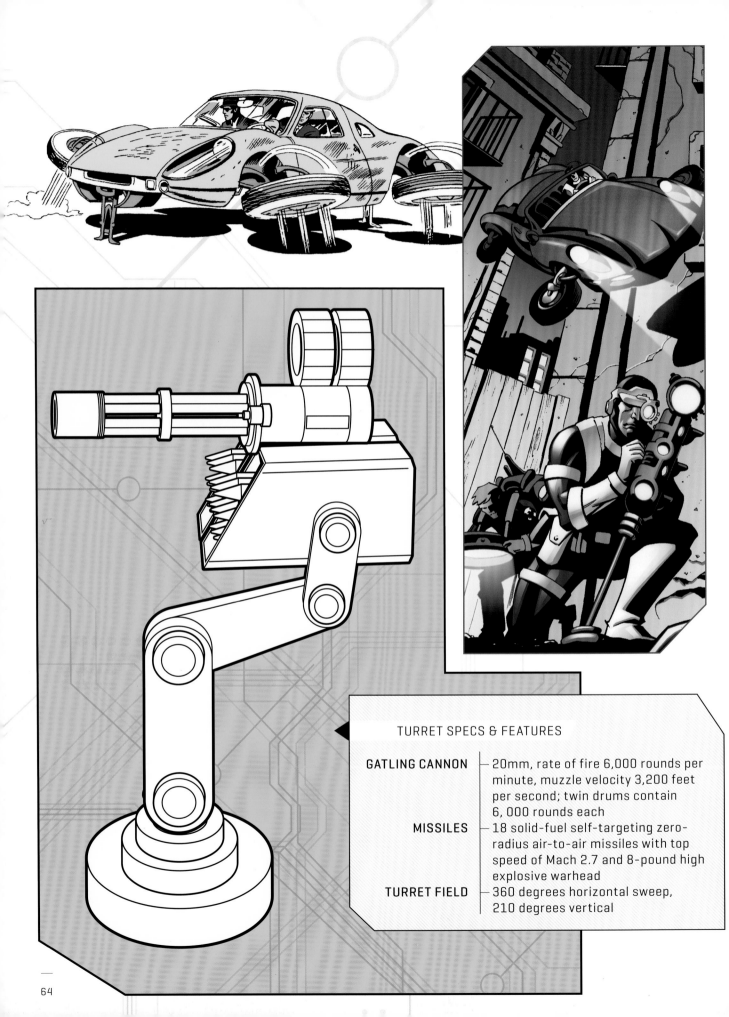

TURRET SPECS & FEATURES

GATLING CANNON	20mm, rate of fire 6,000 rounds per minute, muzzle velocity 3,200 feet per second; twin drums contain 6, 000 rounds each
MISSILES	18 solid-fuel self-targeting zero-radius air-to-air missiles with top speed of Mach 2.7 and 8-pound high explosive warhead
TURRET FIELD	360 degrees horizontal sweep, 210 degrees vertical

NICK FURY

The flying car also can operate underwater for several hours. The passenger cabin is hermetically sealed, and an internal air supply activates automatically when the car submerges. The car is also capable of landing on water with the aid of flotation collars housed along the edges of the undercarriage; these also serve as emergency surfacing assistance in the event of subsurface damage or mechanical failure. Certain variant versions of the vehicle were equipped with holographic projectors that could give them the appearance of any model of car. Other camouflage technologies include multiple license plates and photovoltaic-activated paint that can be changed to any color.

OPPOSITE TOP: The flying car is constantly adapted to mirror trends in civilian vehicle design to ensure it can always blend into traffic when needed.
TOP: The flying car is seen here at an altitude of several thousand feet, near its operational flight ceiling.

I FIRST TOOK A RIDE IN A FLYING CAR BEFORE I EVEN KNEW THERE WAS A S.H.I.E.L.D. THAT'S HOW STARK STARTED MY INTERVIEW, IF YOU CAN CALL IT THAT. TYPICAL TONY STARK, SETTING EVERYTHING UP JUST HOW HE WANTS IT FOR MAXIMUM IMPACT. SINCE THEN I'VE PROBABLY PUT IN TEN THOUSAND HOURS IN EVERY MODEL OF THE CAR WE'VE EVER COMMISSIONED. YOU CAN'T BEAT THEM FOR MISSIONS WHERE YOU NEED TO BE SOMEWHERE FAST BUT DON'T WANT TO MAKE A FUSS WHEN YOU ARRIVE. WHEN THE BAD GUYS ARE LOOKING FOR A QUINJET OR ONE OF S.H.I.E.L.D.'S HEAVY AIRCRAFT, MORE OFTEN THAN NOT YOU CAN DRIVE RIGHT UP TO THEM IN A CAR AND THEY NEVER KNOW YOU'RE COMING UNTIL THEY SEE THE S.H.I.E.L.D. LOGO ON YOUR UNIFORM. IT ALSO DOESN'T HURT THAT BEING ABLE TO FLY AND OPERATE UNDERWATER MAKES FOR GETAWAY TACTICS NO ENEMY CAN ANTICIPATE.

RUNAWAYS' LEAPFROG

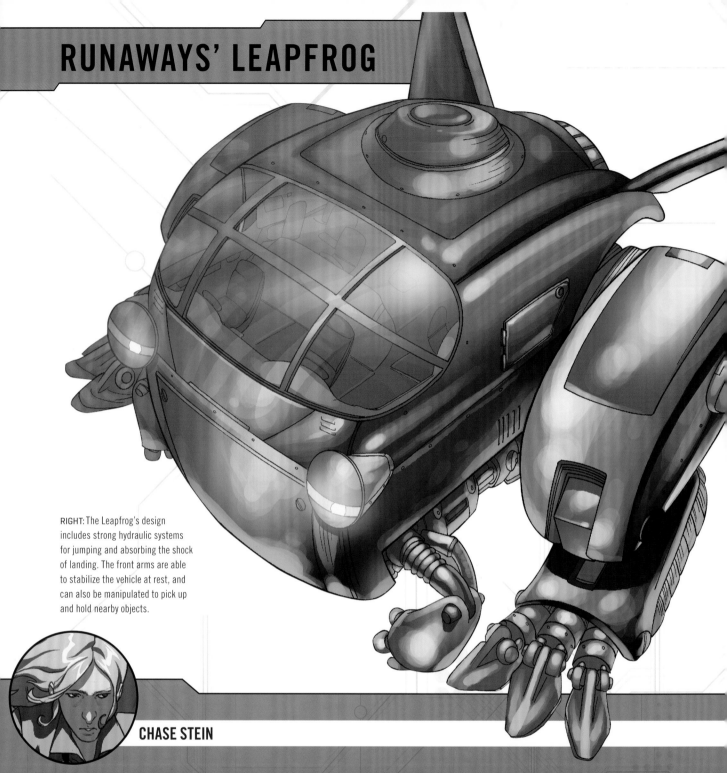

RIGHT: The Leapfrog's design includes strong hydraulic systems for jumping and absorbing the shock of landing. The front arms are able to stabilize the vehicle at rest, and can also be manipulated to pick up and hold nearby objects.

CHASE STEIN

"MY PARENTS BUILT THE LEAPFROG TO GET THEM FROM LOS ANGELES DOWN TO THE VIVARIUM AT THE BOTTOM OF THE OCEAN, WHERE THEY PERFORMED THEIR BLOOD SACRIFICES FOR THE GIBBORIM. AFTER THEY DIED, WE TOOK CONTROL OF THE LEAPFROG. NOW IT'S OURS. IT TALKS TO US, AND I DON'T KNOW ABOUT THE REST OF THE RUNAWAYS, BUT I CONSIDER IT A FRIEND.

THE LEAPFROG CAN'T QUITE FLY, BUT IT CAN JUMP LONG DISTANCES. REALLY LONG DISTANCES. WHEN IT'S IN THE MIDDLE OF A JUMP, YOU MIGHT AS WELL BE FLYING. IT'S GOT AN AI COMMAND SYSTEM THAT CONTROLS ITS LASERS, AND A CLOAKING DEVICE, BOTH OF WHICH COME IN HANDY.

THE OTHER COOL FEATURE OF THE LEAPFROG IS THAT WHEN YOU SLOT THE OVERDRIVE INTO ITS CONTROL PANELS, IT CAN TRAVEL THROUGH TIME. WE'VE ONLY MADE ONE JUMP WITH IT, BACK TO 1907, BUT MY PARENTS WOULDN'T HAVE BUILT THAT FEATURE IF THEY DIDN'T HAVE A REASON. SOMEDAY WE'LL FIGURE OUT WHAT IT WAS."

LEAPING MECHANISM SPECS & FEATURES

LIFTOFF	Initial takeoff achieved by engaging hydraulic piston drives in both legs
LEAP EXTENSION	Rear engine engages as sensors detect leap peak approaching; legs adjust their angles in-flight to maintain stability
RANGE	Engine can extend leap several miles
MAX SPEED	87 mph
MAX ALTITUDE	The Leapfrog can jump more than 1,000 feet straight up with no engine assist
LANDING	Hydraulic piston drives absorb landing impact; Leapfrog can also tilt its body/cabin back at the moment of landing if engine assist is required to lessen landing speed

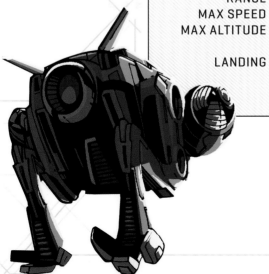

ABOVE: A number of Leapfrog variant designs, housed in a hangar facility belonging to the Wild Pack. LEFT: This posterior view displays the turbojet assist that keeps the Leapfrog in the air longer than unassisted jumping would allow.

LEAPFROG

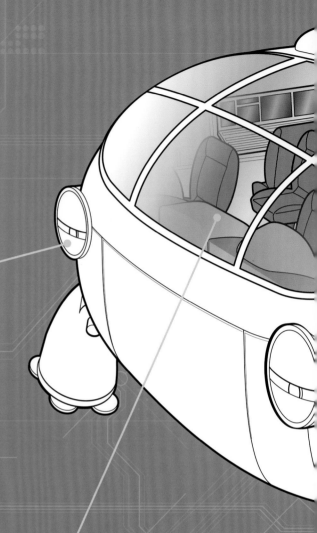

FORWARD-FACING SPOTLIGHTS ADD
TO FROG-THEMED DESIGN

PASSENGER CABIN FEATURES ADVANCED
SURVEILLANCE AND COMMUNICATIONS EQUIPMENT

LEAPFROG SPECS & FEATURES

CREW CAPACITY	10
PROPULSION	"Leaping" by means of galvanic piston-driven leg assemblies
RANGE	"Leaps" extend several miles with assist from rear-facing plasma engine
MULTI-MODAL	Operates in air, on land, and underwater
WEAPONRY	None
OTHER	Cabin-based time-travel matrix generator; other technological capabilities as yet unknown

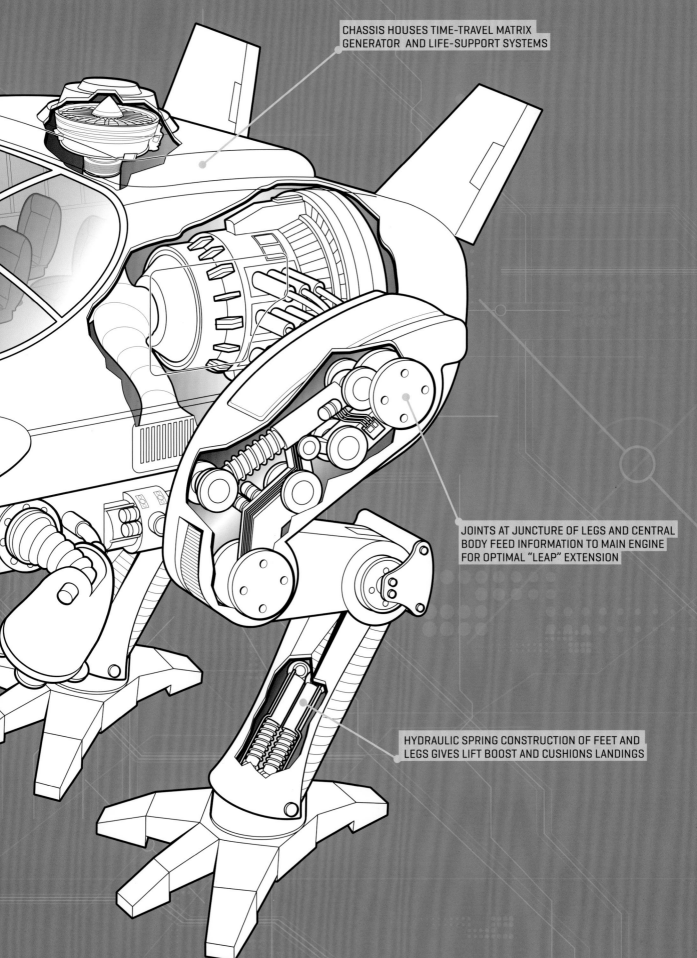

CHASSIS HOUSES TIME-TRAVEL MATRIX
GENERATOR AND LIFE-SUPPORT SYSTEMS

JOINTS AT JUNCTURE OF LEGS AND CENTRAL
BODY FEED INFORMATION TO MAIN ENGINE
FOR OPTIMAL "LEAP" EXTENSION

HYDRAULIC SPRING CONSTRUCTION OF FEET AND
LEGS GIVES LIFT BOOST AND CUSHIONS LANDINGS

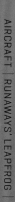

AIRCRAFT | RUNAWAYS' LEAPFROG |

ALPHA FLIGHT OMNIJET

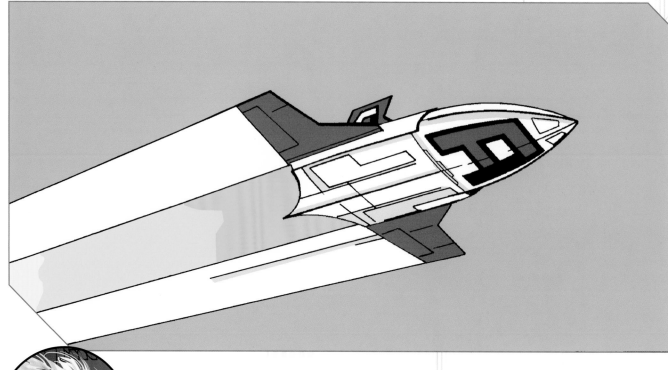

SASQUATCH

ABOVE: The Omnijet, seen here in flight, shares a number of design factors with the Quinjet.
OPPOSITE: The Mooncopter's crescent shape honors Moon Knight's pledge to Khonshu. It also lends itself to closed-rotor stealth propulsion designs, useful for missions requiring the element of surprise.

"I'VE BEEN WITH ALPHA FLIGHT FROM THE BEGINNING, SO I'VE SEEN ALL FOUR ITERATIONS OF THE OMNIJET. THE FIRST ONE WAS PRETTY MUCH A QUINJET WITH A MAPLE LEAF PAINTED ON THE SIDE. IT WAS DESTROYED NOT TOO LONG AFTER DEPARTMENT H HANDED IT OVER TO US FULL-TIME. THE MARK II HAD NEW MODIFICATIONS TO MAKE IT MORE OF A COMBAT FLYER, BUT IT DIDN'T LAST TOO LONG, EITHER. LADY DEATHSTRIKE TOOK IT DOWN WITH SOME KIND OF ELECTROMAGNETIC SWORD.

THE MARK III WAS A GOOD PLANE, A LOT FASTER THAN THE MARK II. WE KEPT WRECKING THEM ON MISSIONS AND MADISON JEFFRIES KEPT PUTTING THEM BACK TOGETHER. HE WAS GOOD AT THAT, WITH HIS METALWORKING POWERS. HE AND BOCHS BROUGHT THE WHOLE TEAM A LONG WAY FORWARD TECHNOLOGICALLY. NOW WE'VE GOT THE MARK IV—SORRY, THE ALPHAJET— AND IT'S GREAT. THERE ARE DIFFERENT VERSIONS FOR DIFFERENT USES—RECONNAISSANCE, COMBAT, FAST TRANSPORT—AND WE FIND WAYS TO USE ALL OF THEM."

ALPHAJET SPECS & FEATURES

- **CREW CAPACITY** 8
- **PROPULSION** Repulsor-ion hybrid yielding 79,000 pounds of thrust; thrust deflectors enable VTOL
- **RANGE** Unlimited
- **MAX SPEED** Mach 2.5
- **MAX ALTITUDE** 84,000 feet
- **WEAPONRY** None standard; variation designed for combat operations features energy weapons and defense systems

MOONCOPTER

MOONCOPTER SPECS & FEATURES

- **CREW CAPACITY** 2
- **PROPULSION** VTOL-capable angled thrusters powered by lens arrays similar to plasma-focused designs prototyped by S.H.I.E.L.D.; closed-rotor assemblies maintain hover with minimal sound
- **RANGE** Unknown
- **MAX SPEED** 160 mph
- **MAX ALTITUDE** 21,000 feet
- **WEAPONRY** Hellfire-class air-to-ground missiles, 30mm chain gun mounted under cockpit, air-to-air battery
- **OTHER FEATURES** Cable spools under dorsal wing surfaces for rappelling; spotlights; nonlethal crowd-control measures; spare costume and personal supplies for Moon Knight

MOON KNIGHT

"WHEN FRENCHIE AND I DECIDED TO GET OUT OF THE MERCENARY LIFE IN AFRICA, WE WANTED TO STICK TOGETHER. THAT'S WHAT COMRADES-IN-ARMS DO. FRENCHIE KNEW MY SECRETS AND I KNEW HIS. WE MADE A GREAT TEAM. HE HAD THE ENGINEERING KNOW-HOW TO BUILD THE FIRST MOONCOPTER FROM THE GROUND UP. I WANTED IT TO LOOK LIKE A CRESCENT MOON, AND HE INTEGRATED THAT INTO THE DESIGN. THEN HE FIGURED OUT HOW TO GET ENOUGH LIFT AND HORIZONTAL THRUST OUT OF A CLOSED-ROTOR DESIGN. THAT FIRST MOONCOPTER WAS A GREAT PIECE OF WORK (S.H.I.E.L.D. EVEN TRIED TO GET ME TO TELL THEM HOW IT WORKED). FRENCHIE DIDN'T STOP THERE, THOUGH. EVEN AFTER HE LOST THE USE OF HIS LEGS, HE KEPT HELPING ME OUT. WE CALLED IN A FEW FAVORS AND GOT HOLD OF SOME SERIOUS ORDNANCE: HELLFIRE MISSILES, A 30-MILLIMETER CHAIN GUN, A BATTERY OF AIR-TO-AIR MISSILES. THE NEXT MOONCOPTER WAS HEAVIER AND MEANER THAN THE FIRST. THE COMMITTEE DIDN'T KNOW WHAT HIT THEM.

BUT WE WEREN'T DONE. AFTER FRENCHIE TRIED OUT CIVILIAN LIFE WITH HIS RESTAURANT, WE GOT BACK TOGETHER. YOU CAN'T GET WAR OUT OF YOUR BLOOD WHEN YOU'RE GUYS LIKE US. WE DESIGNED THE NEW MOONCOPTER WITH VTOL THRUSTERS INSTEAD OF ROTORS AND GAVE IT A NEW DESIGN SO NO MATTER WHAT ANGLE YOU SAW IT FROM, YOU SAW THE MOON. WHEN YOU'RE FIGHTING SCUM AND TERRORISTS WHO LIVE BY SCARING GOOD PEOPLE, THE FIRST THING YOU HAVE TO DO IS MAKE THEM AFRAID OF YOU. THE MOONCOPTER DOES THAT. WHEN YOU SEE IT COMING, YOU KNOW YOU GOT MY ATTENTION. IF YOU'RE A PREDATOR, IF YOU'RE A PERPETRATOR OF INJUSTICE, KHONSHU WILL LEAD ME TO YOU, AND VENGEANCE WILL BE HIS."

THOR'S CHARIOT

ABOVE: The chariot's design is simple, befitting the Asgardian aesthetic. Note the battering ram built onto the front of the yoke holding Toothgrinder and Toothgnasher.

OPPOSITE: The chariot's shape can be adapted to Thor's current needs. Here, it has been reconfigured to feature seats so that Thor can offer a ride to Jane Foster.

DESCRIPTION AND OPERATIONAL HISTORY

Thor's chariot is pulled by two magical goats, Toothgrinder and Toothgnasher, each the size of warhorses. The chariot can ride over any terrain and take to the air on command. It carries no weapons, but Toothgrinder and Toothgnasher strike lightning with their hooves, particularly when they are airborne. Thor can summon and dismiss the chariot at will. For travel on a particular world, Thor typically flies with the aid of Mjolnir, but when it comes to longer voyages, either among Asgardian realms or planets in distant space, he uses the chariot—especially when he anticipates the need to smite an enemy army beneath its wheels. [cont. on p. 76]

THOR'S CHARIOT

"LIGHTNING-RIDER"

THOR'S CHARIOT SPECS & FEATURES

TOOTHGRINDER AND TOOTHGNASHER These two immense goats strike sparks of lightning with their hooves and are part of the chariot's enchantment. They traverse dimensions as easily as they ford rivers.

SCROLLWORK Every part of the chariot is enchanted, including the carvings that decorate its prow and sideboards. Thor is protected from most threats when he stands within, and no others may take the reins . . . even if Toothgrinder and Toothgnasher would let them.

MUTABLE FORM The chariot has changed forms on several occasions. Sometimes it has seats, sometimes an open standing interior. Sometimes it is a single two-wheeled conveyance, other times a train of wagons. The only constant is the goats.

In his youth, Thor drove the chariot between Asgard and Midgard, fighting trolls and other creatures, and later he would ride it into battle against greater foes—notably when he led an Asgardian host against the gods of Olympus to settle a dispute between himself and Hercules. When he is not using the chariot, it remains at an unknown location. The goats—unlike their mythological counterparts, who were cooked and eaten and then brought back to life with Thor's hammer—go out to pasture when Thor has no need of them.

The chariot is capable of traveling through space and among the Nine Realms known to Asgard. It is large enough to carry Thor's companions, as proven when Thor, Sif, and Beta Ray Bill fought Surtur's demon legions in outer space. When Thor went to Hel to recover souls stolen by the dark elf Malekith, the chariot manifested attached wagons to transport many more allies. All of these attachments and modifications can be summoned and dismissed at Thor's command.

FOR HELA BECKONS AND THE HEL-HOUND GARM AWAITS!

THOR

"I HAVE RIDDEN HELICARRIERS AND QUINJETS; CROSSED VAST SPACES THROUGH CRACKS IN THE FABRIC OF SPACE ITSELF; SEEN THE NINE REALMS BY STEPPING THROUGH MAGICAL GATEWAYS; NOTHING, HOWEVER, MATCHES THE FEELING OF TOOTHGRINDER AND TOOTHGNASHER STRAINING AT THE REINS OF MY CHARIOT AS WE HURTLE AMONG WORLDS AND DRIVE FORWARD INTO BATTLE. I HAVE CRUSHED JOTUN AND DARK ELVES UNDER ITS WHEELS, RACED OVER BIFROST TIMES BEYOND NUMBER, AND FACED DOWN THE SHIELD-WALL OF HEL IN THE LAND OF THE DEAD.

THE CHARIOT HAS ALSO BROUGHT ME TO WISDOM. DURING THE TWILIGHT OF THE GODS, AFTER MY FATHER DIED, A STRANGE BOY APPEARED. TO UNDERSTAND HIM, AND WHAT ROLE HE WOULD PLAY IN THE EVENTS TO COME, I DROVE THE CHARIOT TO HLIDSKJALF, MY FATHER'S HIGH THRONE. FROM THERE A WATCHER CAN SEE ALL THAT HAPPENS IN THE NINE REALMS. ODIN ONCE SACRIFICED ONE OF HIS EYES FOR WISDOM, AND AT HLIDSKJALF, I SURRENDERED BOTH OF MINE, LEARNING IN RETURN THAT THE BOY WAS A WALKING AVATAR OF THE ODINFORCE. BUT I ALSO LEARNED THAT I WAS TO DIE. HAD I NOT POSSESSED THE CHARIOT, I COULD NEVER HAVE MADE THAT VOYAGE IN TIME TO ACT ON THE KNOWLEDGE GAINED. ASGARD STILL STANDS BECAUSE TOOTHGRINDER AND TOOTHGNASHER REMAIN EVER AT THE READY."

DEADPOOL CORPS' BEA ARTHUR

ABOVE: Bea Arthur featured complete life-support systems for spacewalks, which came in handy for recovering severed heads.

BEA ARTHUR SPECS & FEATURES

CREW CAPACITY	Me, and whoever else. Mostly me.
ENGINE	The big thing with the spinny parts and the fire coming out the back. Seriously, you didn't know that?
RANGE	Dunno, but I went to a couple other planets, so, you know, light-years.
MAX SPEED	FASTER THAN YOU!
WEAPONRY	I was on board. She didn't need any.
OTHER FEATURES	EVERYTHING YOU COULD EVER WANT AND IF YOU SAY OTHERWISE I'M GONNA . . . okay. Nevermind. She was a great ship. I don't get sentimental about too much, but I miss her. She had a cool spot for me to put all my little yellow boxes when I wasn't using them.

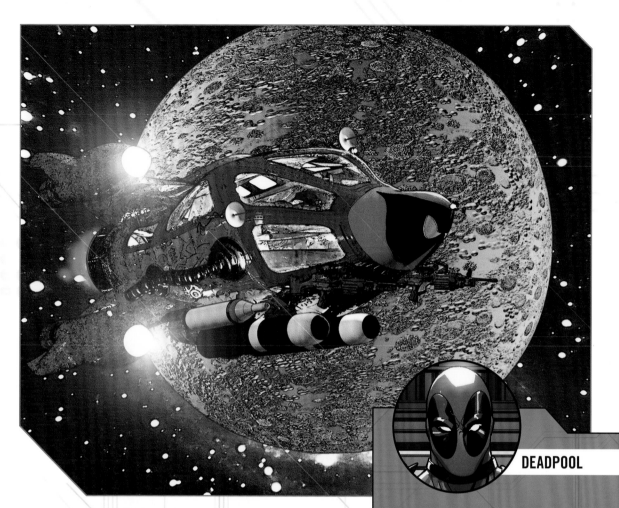

TOP: Bea Arthur didn't just fight in near-Earth space. Here she is, carrying the Deadpool Corps on a mission into deep space.
ABOVE: Bea Arthur is seen here facing down an interstellar armada during the battle against the Awareness.

DEADPOOL

"I LOVE BEA ARTHUR. I LOVE HER LIKE I LOVE CHIMICHANGAS AND SUCKING CHEST WOUNDS. YOU LOVE BEA ARTHUR, TOO, RIGHT? YOU BETTER. I LOVE HER SO MUCH I NAMED A SHIP AFTER HER. WE—I MEAN ALL THE OTHER DEADPOOLS—USED IT TO FIGHT THE MIGHTY AWARENESS! THE AWARENESS NEVER HAD A CHANCE AGAINST US, BECAUSE ALL IT CAN DO IS DEVOUR CONSCIOUSNESS AND NONE OF US ARE EXACTLY WHAT YOU'D CALL CONSCIOUS. OR AWARE. SO WE DID IT IN, AND DID OUR PART TO MAKE THE UNIVERSE A LITTLE LESS AWARE. THEN DREADPOOL HAD TO START SOME SHIZZLE, TRYING TO KILL ALL OF THE DEADPOOL CORPS. WE WENT AFTER HIM, AND EVERYTHING WOULD HAVE BEEN HUNKY-DORY EXCEPT HE BROUGHT IN GALACTIPOOL. PARTY FOUL. THE ONLY WAY TO TAKE HIM DOWN WAS TO SACRIFICE ALL THAT WAS DEAREST TO US . . . BY WHICH I MEAN LADY DEADPOOL CRASHED THE BEA ARTHUR INTO HIS HEAD. I KINDA MISS HER. I MEAN LADY DEADPOOL. BUT I REALLY, REALLY, REALLY MISS BEA ARTHUR. I MEAN THE SHIP. BUT THE REAL ONE, TOO. WHAT A LADY."

GLIDERS

GOBLIN GLIDER

ABOVE: The Goblin Glider gives the Green Goblin a solid footing for accurate hurling of pumpkin bombs.

OPPOSITE: The turbofan intake is set behind the Glider's figurehead and amplifies the Glider's thrust power while channeling thrust through deflector ducts for quick changes of direction.

DESCRIPTION AND OPERATIONAL HISTORY

The Goblin Glider is a highly maneuverable, rocket-driven sled created by inventor and industrialist Norman Osborn, also known as the Green Goblin. The Goblin Glider can reach approximately 90 miles per hour, but is often used at lower speeds. It can hover using deflector ducts that channel exhaust downward at variable angles and intensities from ports below the base of each wing. Its fuel capacity is sufficient to keep it in the air for an hour, dependent on speed. Higher velocities consume fuel more rapidly, although the construction of the rocket engine is such that its baseline consumption is fairly high compared to full thrust. As a result of this, the Glider's peak consumption is less than fifty percent higher than idling/hovering

burn rates. Hovering requires as much energy as flying at medium speeds, since the Glider cannot take advantage of lift from its wings while it is hovering.

The Glider's aerial maneuverability and small size make it ideally suited for the confined interior and urban spaces where it is normally used. Others utilized the Glider when Osborn was still active as the Green Goblin, some adapting Osborn's original design for their own purposes. All have stayed close to the fundamentals of the original Glider, suggesting Osborn had already come close to optimizing the Goblin Glider when the vehicle began its operational life.

The first-generation Goblin Glider was nimble enough to keep up with Spider-Man and had automatic homing sensors that returned it to the Green Goblin whenever they were separated. *[cont. on p. 88]*

GOBLIN GLIDER
POST-THUNDERBOLTS 2013 MODEL

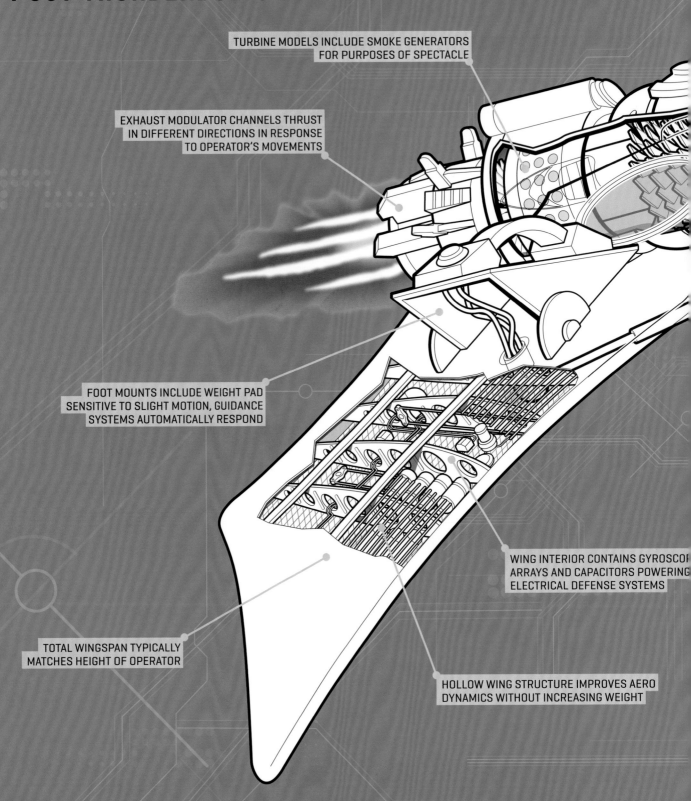

TURBINE MODELS INCLUDE SMOKE GENERATORS FOR PURPOSES OF SPECTACLE

EXHAUST MODULATOR CHANNELS THRUST IN DIFFERENT DIRECTIONS IN RESPONSE TO OPERATOR'S MOVEMENTS

FOOT MOUNTS INCLUDE WEIGHT PAD SENSITIVE TO SLIGHT MOTION, GUIDANCE SYSTEMS AUTOMATICALLY RESPOND

WING INTERIOR CONTAINS GYROSCOP ARRAYS AND CAPACITORS POWERING ELECTRICAL DEFENSE SYSTEMS

TOTAL WINGSPAN TYPICALLY MATCHES HEIGHT OF OPERATOR

HOLLOW WING STRUCTURE IMPROVES AERO DYNAMICS WITHOUT INCREASING WEIGHT

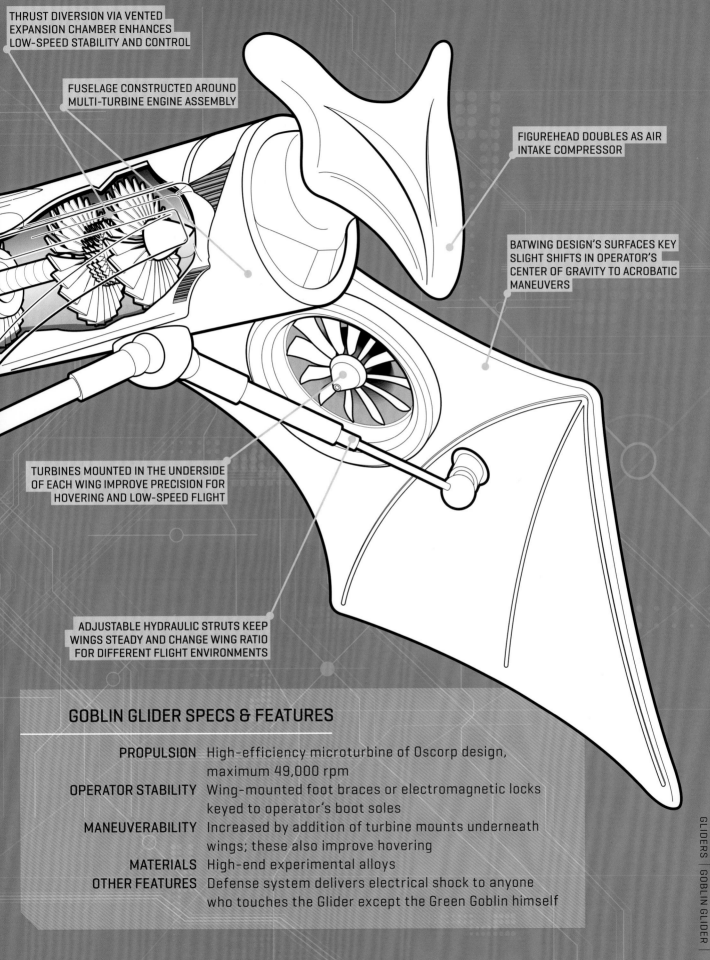

THRUST DIVERSION VIA VENTED
EXPANSION CHAMBER ENHANCES
LOW-SPEED STABILITY AND CONTROL

FUSELAGE CONSTRUCTED AROUND
MULTI-TURBINE ENGINE ASSEMBLY

FIGUREHEAD DOUBLES AS AIR
INTAKE COMPRESSOR

BATWING DESIGN'S SURFACES KEY
SLIGHT SHIFTS IN OPERATOR'S
CENTER OF GRAVITY TO ACROBATIC
MANEUVERS

TURBINES MOUNTED IN THE UNDERSIDE
OF EACH WING IMPROVE PRECISION FOR
HOVERING AND LOW-SPEED FLIGHT

ADJUSTABLE HYDRAULIC STRUTS KEEP
WINGS STEADY AND CHANGE WING RATIO
FOR DIFFERENT FLIGHT ENVIRONMENTS

GOBLIN GLIDER SPECS & FEATURES

PROPULSION	High-efficiency microturbine of Oscorp design, maximum 49,000 rpm
OPERATOR STABILITY	Wing-mounted foot braces or electromagnetic locks keyed to operator's boot soles
MANEUVERABILITY	Increased by addition of turbine mounts underneath wings; these also improve hovering
MATERIALS	High-end experimental alloys
OTHER FEATURES	Defense system delivers electrical shock to anyone who touches the Glider except the Green Goblin himself

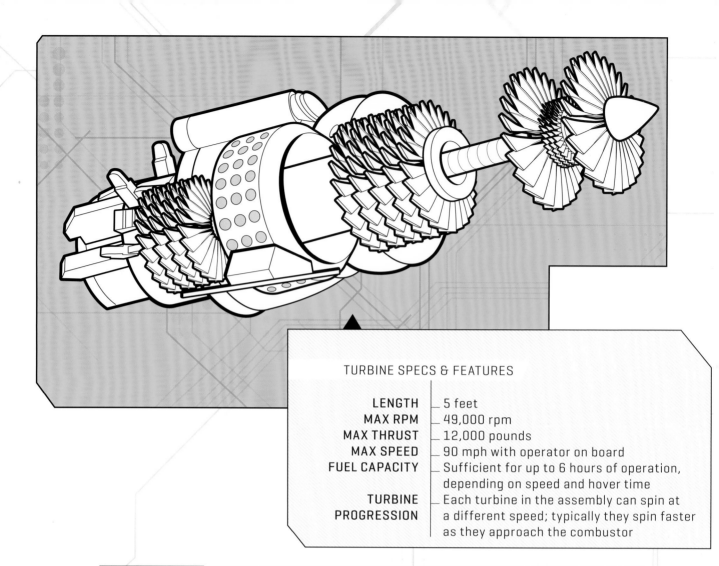

TURBINE SPECS & FEATURES

LENGTH	5 feet
MAX RPM	49,000 rpm
MAX THRUST	12,000 pounds
MAX SPEED	90 mph with operator on board
FUEL CAPACITY	Sufficient for up to 6 hours of operation, depending on speed and hover time
TURBINE PROGRESSION	Each turbine in the assembly can spin at a different speed; typically they spin faster as they approach the combustor

It could also be used as a simple battering ram and had a robust gyroscopic assembly capable of controlling direction and velocity after impact. These early Gliders lacked storage capacity, requiring the Green Goblin to carry a satchel for his personal arsenal of pumpkin bombs.

It was also strong enough to carry the mass of another person. The Goblin Glider carried Gwen Stacy to the top of the George Washington Bridge, where she fell to her death, despite Spider-Man's desperate rescue efforts. In the ensuing battle, Spider-Man held himself back from killing the Goblin, but the Goblin Glider's automated remote recall itself became a lethal weapon, skewering the green-skinned villain.

Neither the Green Goblin nor the Glider were permanently out of commission. A number of Goblins succeeded Osborn, beginning with his son Harry, before Osborn himself reassumed the role. Each improved the technology of the Goblin Glider. Later iterations included more sophisticated electronics, controlled from a small assembly set behind the Glider's head. While early versions were controlled almost entirely by the Green Goblin shifting his weight and increasing or decreasing thrust, later upgrades to the Glider included voice control. The rider of the early Gliders set their feet into stirrups built on the wingtips, but later advances used electromagnetic locks to keep the rider's feet set. These could be released at will.

When Osborn assumed control of the Thunderbolts—a team of (mostly) reformed villains—he was still keeping the Green Goblin gear stowed away and his alter ego under wraps. His unbalanced psyche gradually tipped back in the direction of the Goblin, and he went on a rampage through Thunderbolts Mountain riding an updated Goblin Glider. This Glider differed in some key design elements from earlier versions, most notably in the glowing eyes that replaced the featureless goblin-head shape of the Green Goblin's first Gliders. It retained the trademark batwing shape and the single rocket exhaust.

TOP: The Glider used in Osborn's Thunderbolts Mountain rampage. Note the compact profile and closed-rotor secondary motors for altitude control.
ABOVE: Norman Osborn, seen here shortly before he brought the Goblin Glider out of storage and ran amok in Thunderbolts Mountain.

JACK O'LANTERN'S POGO PLATFORM

POGO PLATFORM SPECS & FEATURES

DIAMETER	36 inches
MAX CAPACITY	300 pounds
POGO	True to its name, the Pogo Platform was not designed to fly. Instead, it was able to bounce off any surface at any angle while maintaining its rider's balance
FULL HOVER	To create the Pogo Platform, Jack O'Lantern reverse engineered the other Gliders he observed

SPIDER-MAN

"MACHINE MAN RAN INTO JACK O'LANTERN BEFORE I DID, SO HE WAS THE LUCKY GUY WHO FIRST SAW THE POGO PLATFORM. THAT WAS TWO OR THREE JACK O'LANTERNS AGO, BACK WHEN JASON MACENDALE WAS STILL JACK AND HADN'T GONE OFF AND SOLD HIS SOUL TO THE DEMON WHO LATER USED HIM TO CREATE DEMOGOBLIN. THAT'S ANOTHER STORY. MACENDALE WAS AN ENGINEERING GENIUS, AND HE BUILT THE POGO PLATFORM TO FLY, WHICH IS A PRETTY GOOD TRICK ALL BY ITSELF—BUT HE ALSO HAD A SPHERICAL STRUCTURE ON THE BOTTOM OF IT THAT LET HIM SKIP AND BOUNCE OFF HARD SURFACES. THAT MADE HIM PRETTY HARD TO GET A BEAD ON, BECAUSE JUST WHEN YOU THOUGHT HE WAS GOING TOO FAST AND WAS ABOUT TO CRASH INTO SOMETHING—BOING! OFF HE'D GO IN ANOTHER DIRECTION. WHEN I FOUGHT JACK O'LANTERN, I ALWAYS TRIED TO GET HIM OFF THE PLATFORM. ONCE HE WAS ON THE GROUND HE WAS A LOT EASIER TO HANDLE. MACENDALE'S DEAD NOW, BUT WHATEVER LOON IS NOW USING THE JACK O'LANTERN IDENTITY STILL HAS THE POGO PLATFORM."

SPIDER-GLIDER

SPIDER-MAN

SPIDER-GLIDER SPECS & FEATURES

— **PROPULSION** A number of distributed repulsor-lift thrusters modulate exhaust in response to operator commands

— **CONTROL** Spider-Man controls the Spider-Glider by shifting his feet, the motion automatically transmitting instructions to the flight-control system

— **SPIDER-SHAPE** Eight legs and a rounded body replace the common batwing chassis

— **MANDATORY SATCHEL** Like the Green Goblin and Hobgoblin, Spider-Man wears a satchel full of dangerous projectiles when he's on the Spider-Glider

OPPOSITE: Jack O'Lantern seen operating the Pogo Platform. Internal gyroscopes keep it level during jumps.
ABOVE: The Spider-Glider incorporates a design and color scheme recalling Spider-Man's famous logo.

"HORIZON LABS IS A GEARHEAD'S DREAMLAND. I WAS FIGURING THAT SINCE I SPEND ALL THIS TIME CHASING AFTER BAD GUYS WHO HAVE THEIR OWN GLIDERS, WHY NOT MAKE ONE OF MY OWN? I USED THE GOBLIN GLIDER AS A PROTOTYPE, AND PRETTY SOON I HAD A SPIDER-GLIDER, MY VERY OWN AERIAL TRANSPORT. GOBBIE'S WAS A BATWING KIND OF DESIGN WITH A GOBLIN HEAD, WHICH DIDN'T WORK FOR ME, SO I BUILT MINE IN THE SHAPE OF-YOU GUESSED IT-A SPIDER. YOU GOTTA STAY TRUE TO YOUR NATURE.

I EVEN PICKED UP ON GOBBIE'S PREFERRED METHOD OF CARRYING HIS LITTLE PUMPKIN BOMBS AND GOT MYSELF A SATCHEL FOR SOME THROWN FIREWORKS OF MY OWN . . . WELL, NOT EXACTLY FIREWORKS. THERMOREACTIVE FOAM BOMBLETS, WHICH ARE KIND OF ANTI-FIREWORKS. I DESIGNED THEM SPECIFICALLY TO HANDLE EQUINOX, AND THEY WORKED LIKE A CHARM. I STILL PREFER WEB-SLINGING AND WALL-CRAWLING TO GET FROM POINT A TO POINT B, BUT I HAVE TO ADMIT, SOMETIMES IT'S PRETTY COOL TO ZIP AROUND THE CITY ON A GLIDER."

HOBGOBLIN GLIDER

ABOVE: The Hobgoblin Glider seen here features both the rear rocket thruster and under-wing directional stabilizers. Note also the Hobgoblin's adaptation of the Green Goblin's original figurehead.

OPPOSITE: The sleeker profile, including rounded wing surfaces and a flatter figurehead angle, made this Hobgoblin Glider better suited for punching through certain obstacles without losing flight stability.

During the Green Goblin's period of inactivity, the costume, gear, and Glider remained in an underground facility below the shuttered Osborn Manufacturing facility. That is, until George Hill, a bank robber on the run from Spider-Man, found his way into Osborn's hideout and started looking around for someone who might want to buy the Green Goblin's old equipment. The buyer, deranged billionaire Roderick Kingsley, became the first Hobgoblin and used Osborn's Glider as a template for his own innovations.

The Hobgoblin Glider had significantly upgraded lift and thrust powers, as Spider-Man himself found out. It was also just as quick and elusive as Osborn's original, and surprisingly robust—although Spider-Man did once damage it.

Other Hobgoblins—notably the gifted engineer Jason Macendale—made their own improvements to Osborn's original design. Macendale's Hobgoblin added an array of directional thrusters enabling reverse flight, as well as surface-conducted electrical weaponry that would electrocute anyone who touched the Glider—and prevent the victim from letting go. Since the original Green Goblin used electrically charged gauntlets as a short-range weapon, this system was likely a derivative of the early technology.

DEMOGOBLIN GLIDER

During Jason Macendale's tenure as Hobgoblin, he made a deal with a demon and then struggled to separate himself from the demonic aspects of his personality and soul. A demonic entity known as Demogoblin later split off from Macendale. Demogoblin piloted his own glider, visually reminiscent of previous glider designs. This one, true to its rider's demonic nature, was composed of hellfire, with no visible power source. It is not known whether this hellfire is the same substance infusing Ghost Rider's motorcycle.

SPIDER-MAN

"IF YOU'RE LOOKING FOR MY TYPICAL WALL-CRAWLING WISECRACKS HERE, SORRY TO DISAPPOINT. WHEN I SEE ANY OF THESE NUTJOBS ON A GLIDER, I REMEMBER GWEN . . . THAT'S THE THING ABOUT THESE GUYS. THEY GO AFTER WHAT'S DEAREST TO YOU, BECAUSE THEY WANT YOU TO TURN INTO A LOON LIKE THEM. WHEN GWEN DIED, I ALMOST SNAPPED AND KILLED THE GREEN GOBLIN, BUT I REELED MYSELF BACK IN AT THE LAST MINUTE BECAUSE I FIGURED SOMETHING OUT. WANT TO KNOW WHAT? SIMPLE. I DIDN'T WANT TO BE A KILLER. GOBBIE, HOBBIE, AND EVEN JACK O'LANTERN GET OFF ON IT. THEY DON'T EVEN KNOW WHO THEY ARE, WHAT WITH ALL THE IDENTITY-SWAPPING AND EVERYTHING ELSE, BUT THEY HAVE TWO THINGS IN COMMON. THEY LIKE KILLING, AND THEY ALL HAVE TO USE GLIDERS.

WHICH MEANS I HAVE LOTS OF EXPERIENCE WITH THEM. I CAN TELL YOU THEY'RE QUICK ENOUGH THAT EVEN I CAN'T ALWAYS GET A BEAD ON THEM WITH MY LITTLE OL' WEB-SHOOTERS. SOMETIMES IT'S EASIER TO WATCH THE RIDER IF YOU WANT TO ANTICIPATE WHERE THE GLIDER'S GOING TO GO; ALL OF THEM STILL STEER BY SHIFTS IN WEIGHT, SO WHEN YOU LEARN TO LOOK FOR LITTLE MOTIONS IN THE LEGS, YOU'VE GOT THE UPPER HAND. THAT HELPS YOU KEEP AWAY FROM ALL THE ELECTRICAL SAPPY STUFF THOSE LOONS LIKE TO BUILD INTO THE SLEDS. ONCE YOU KNOCK THEM OFF, THE ODDS ARE EVENED UP.

I ALSO LEARNED FROM WATCHING THEM FIGHT EACH OTHER. I'VE SEEN HOBGOBLIN TAKE ON JACK O'LANTERN, AND GOBBIE TAKE ON HOBGOBLIN-EXCEPT I THINK IT WAS A DIFFERENT HOBGOBLIN. WHO CAN KEEP THEM STRAIGHT? ANYWAY, WHEN YOU WATCH THEM ON GLIDERS FIGHTING EACH OTHER YOU START TO SEE THE LITTLE DIFFERENCES. LIKE THE ONES WITH ELECTROMAGNETIC FOOT LOCKS VERSUS THE ACTUAL LOOPS, OR THE ONES WITH OLD-FASHIONED SOLID-FUEL ROCKET ENGINES RATHER THAN THE NEW PLASMA PROPULSION SYSTEMS . . . I FILE IT ALL AWAY, BECAUSE SOONER OR LATER I'M GOING TO RUN INTO ONE OF THEM AGAIN."

MENACE GLIDER

OPPOSITE: Demogoblin's Glider almost appeared to have an infernal life of its own, as evidenced by the fiery claws and monstrous head seen here.

ABOVE: The version of the Glider briefly controlled by Menace showcased a much slimmer flight profile and greater wingspan than many of its predecessors. Note also the open figurehead rather than the traditional bat- or goblin-head design.

While Norman Osborn was in charge of the Thunderbolts, the villain Menace adopted the look of the Green Goblin and liberated one of Osborn's Gliders. After a brief struggle during which Menace tried to spear Osborn with his own Glider, Osborn turned the tables, taking control of the Glider remotely and using it to defeat Menace. Other Glider designs have continued to incorporate flight-command subsystems for limited autonomy and automated recall to the operator's location.

SPACESHIPS

THANOS' SANCTUARY CLASS SHIP

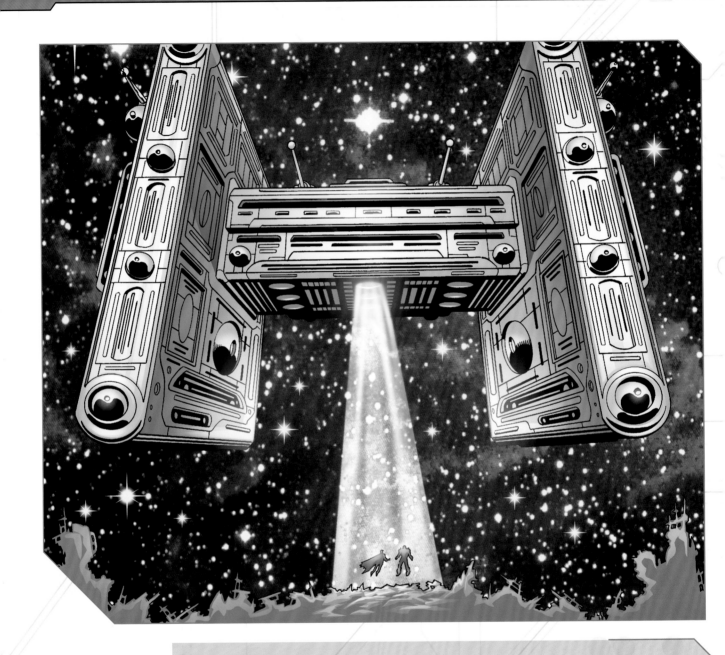

ABOVE: Tractor beams are only one of the highly advanced technologies built into Sanctuary-class starships.
OPPOSITE: A Sanctuary-class ship is destroyed during one of Thanos' attempts to harness the powers of the infinite.

DESCRIPTION AND OPERATIONAL HISTORY

A number of immense spaceships have borne the name Sanctuary, but one in particular, known as Sanctuary II, has been Thanos' preferred means of interstellar transport for decades. Little is known of the others beyond the fact of their existence. Each was constructed by Thanos to be his capital ship. The Avengers first learned of Sanctuary-class starships when Adam Warlock detected the use of one of the ships' ion laser signature weapons, the Star-Burster. This ion laser beam projector is powered by the Star Gem, a synthetic crystal created from elements of the other Infinity Gems. The Star-Burster unbalances the internal fusion equilibrium of a star, causing it to go through the final stages of its life cycle in hours rather than billions of years. With it, Thanos has destroyed stars beyond count. [cont. on p. 102]

SANCTUARY II

DORSAL VENTS RADIATE WASTE HEAT FROM PLASMA CORE AND KEEP SHIP'S INTERNAL TEMPERATURE STABLE

HYPERSPACE ENGINE TAPS SEPARATE POWER SUPPLY FROM PLASMA CORE

DEFENSE SYSTEMS PROTECT REAR HANGAR BAY WHICH HOUSES AN UNKNOWN NUMBER OF SPACECRAFT

SANCTUARY SPECS & FEATURES

DIMENSIONS	Roughly 2,000 feet in length and width; height approximately 1,000 feet from base of hull to tip or antenna arrays
MASS	Approximately 500,000 tons
PROPULSION	Ionized plasma engines designed by Thanos; hyperspace transit accomplished by means of Thanos' own powers or onboard subspace collapsar engine
RANGE	Unlimited via both normal space flight and hyperspace transit
DEFENSE SYSTEMS	Energy shielding powered by plasma core; onboard AI response counters and repels infiltration or direct assault within the ship itself
WEAPONRY	Robot drone force; thermonuclear missiles; Star-Burster ion laser cannon

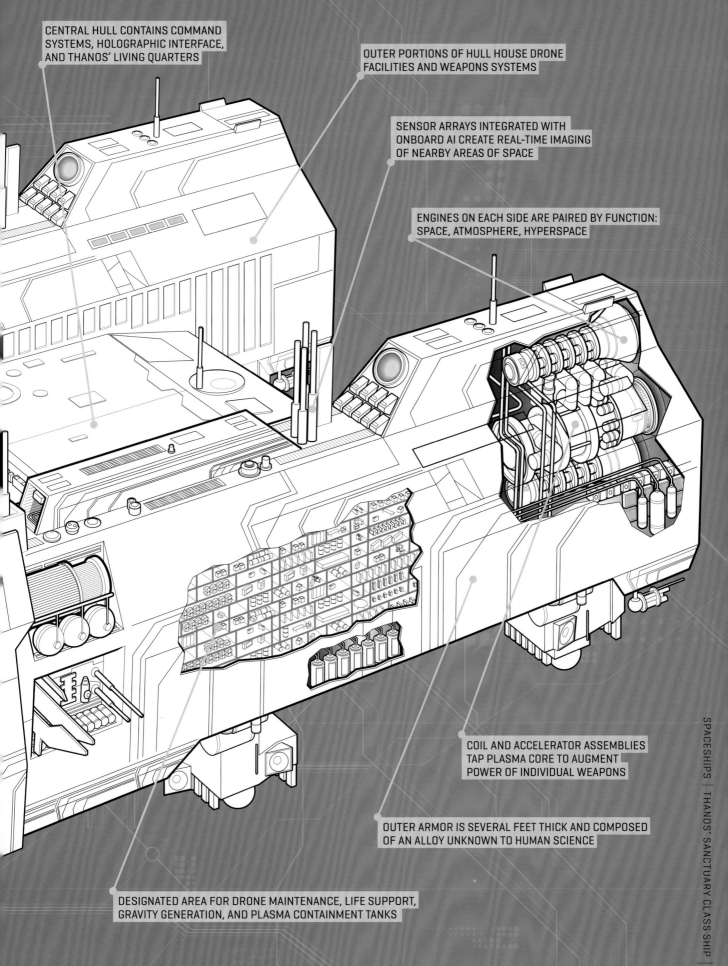

CENTRAL HULL CONTAINS COMMAND SYSTEMS, HOLOGRAPHIC INTERFACE, AND THANOS' LIVING QUARTERS

OUTER PORTIONS OF HULL HOUSE DRONE FACILITIES AND WEAPONS SYSTEMS

SENSOR ARRAYS INTEGRATED WITH ONBOARD AI CREATE REAL-TIME IMAGING OF NEARBY AREAS OF SPACE

ENGINES ON EACH SIDE ARE PAIRED BY FUNCTION: SPACE, ATMOSPHERE, HYPERSPACE

COIL AND ACCELERATOR ASSEMBLIES TAP PLASMA CORE TO AUGMENT POWER OF INDIVIDUAL WEAPONS

OUTER ARMOR IS SEVERAL FEET THICK AND COMPOSED OF AN ALLOY UNKNOWN TO HUMAN SCIENCE

DESIGNATED AREA FOR DRONE MAINTENANCE, LIFE SUPPORT, GRAVITY GENERATION, AND PLASMA CONTAINMENT TANKS

Sanctuary II features a hangar with the capacity to hold hundreds of spacecraft. Most of these ships are piloted by the robotic drones Thanos maintains as crew and cannon fodder. Storage and maintenance facilities for the drones and Sanctuary II's systems take up another large part of the interior, but the ship's size is such that no single person has ever seen all of it. Captain Marvel, one of the first explorers, remarked that all of New Orleans and half of Baton Rouge would fit inside.

Surprisingly little of that vast space is dedicated to engines, reactors, and fuel tanks. As Sanctuary does not rely on acceleration or maneuverability, a single plasma core is enough to power the entire ship. In space, near planets, it moves slowly. When Thanos desires for the ship to be elsewhere, he utilizes either Sanctuary's embedded faster-than-light technology or the interface hardwired with his own powers of teleportation. Sanctuary's power systems contribute to an energy field matrix that not only enhances Thanos' powers, but also allows him to control the ship with his thoughts.

Sanctuary's command systems can be very difficult for human minds to understand. Projected in a column from floor to ceiling, in the center of a bridge the size of the Helicarrier's flight deck, is a holographic representation of several thousand nearby stars. These interact with the onboard artificial intelligence to give the ship—and therefore Thanos—real-time information about everything happening within ten light-years. Sanctuary's computer systems have an unlimited capacity to track, target, and intercept approaching spacecraft.

On a wall of holographic displays, Thanos has access to a near-universal library of information on civilizations, technology, and galactic history. From the bridge, he can teleport at will to any location in the universe by locking onto it via these holographic displays, an action he can perform either by direct input or by mental command. Sanctuary's systems are fully psionically capable, and in many ways, the ship is an extension of Thanos' mind.

ABOVE: Sanctuary II's size becomes apparent in this image, with other combat spacecraft visible for comparison.

ABOVE: This newest version of the Sanctuary-class ship, seen during Thanos' search for his son Thane, is observed here from the rear, displaying plasma exhaust from its engines.

Defense systems on Sanctuary-class ships include a force field powerful enough to resist all but stellar energies. This force field also returns energies directed at it, becoming a reactionary offensive force. When the ship detects a weakening in one part of the force field, energy can quickly be redirected to that area. The shield can also be deliberately overloaded from within, causing it to shed excess energy in a blast wave that damages or destroys all nearby machines and life-forms. Used merely for defense, Sanctuary's shields can absorb the full onslaught of fleet sorties from advanced civilizations such as Rigel-3.

The Star-Burster is not Sanctuary's only planetary-class weapon. It carries thermonuclear missiles—a primitive technology by Thanos' standards, but an effective weapon, and the one he used to destroy his homeworld. It has little in the way of anti-ship weapons as Thanos does not believe Sanctuary needs them. The ship is protected by layers of physical armor, squadrons of robot drones, and internal defense systems.

More than once Thanos has used Sanctuary as his base of operations for large-scale campaigns of conquest. Most recently, with his cadre of lieutenants known as the Cull Obsidian, or Black Order, he piloted Sanctuary across the stars in search of his last surviving child, Thane. This campaign demonstrated Sanctuary's symbolic value, terrorizing populations and serving as a visible reminder of the immense power of the "Mad Titan."

FLYING THRONE

FLYING THRONE SPECS & FEATURES

— **PROPULSION SYSTEM** Unknown;
was suspected to be a manifestation
of Thanos' powers
— **WEAPONRY** None known
— **INTELLIGENCE GATHERING** Armpad
quantum-field sensors could detect
individual energy signature of any
sentient being
— **DIMENSION SHIFT** Flying Throne could
travel among dimensions as quickly as
it could traverse interstellar distances

Thanos' Flying Throne was a personal transport in the
shape of an ornate metallic dais and chair. Despite its
unremarkable appearance, its powers were incredible.
Simply by resting his palm on a sensor pad located on one
arm of the Throne, Thanos could search out the individual
subatomic vibrational signature of any sentient being or
any object. The Flying Throne could also travel interstellar
distances almost instantaneously, and demonstrated
the capacity to shift through dimensions as well. It was
destroyed by the Runner while Thanos was searching
for the Infinity Gems.

DREADNOUGHT 666

With a design that recalls a gun barrel, Dreadnought's bow section was entirely given over to the enormous discharge ports of its main energy weapons. From its bridge, Thanos could track the energy signatures and psionic patterns of individual targets. Its visual sensors were acute enough to provide Thanos with visual confirmation when he located Gamora on Paradise Omega and used the Dreadnought's main battery of weapons to vaporize part of the planet's surface. This attack revealed a weakness in the Dreadnought's design, however. Shielding around the target location reflected the beam's energy, setting up a resonance within the discharge chambers that destroyed the ship—or so it seemed at the time.

DREADNOUGHT SPECS & FEATURES

- **DIMENSIONS** Approximately 3,000 feet long, 1,000 feet high, 300 feet wide
- **SYSTEMS CONTROL** Quantum-field sweep analysis capable of locating individuals anywhere within several light-years
- **WEAPONRY** Planetary-scale energy weapons housed in the ship's front face

GUARDIANS OF THE GALAXY SHIP

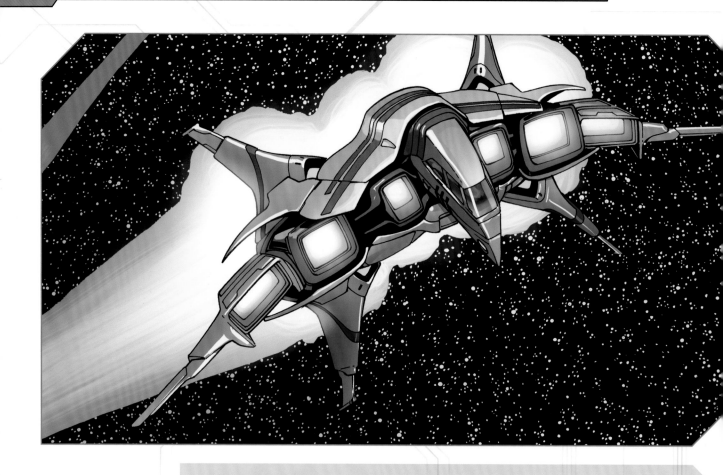

ABOVE: Six ion scoops power both the ship's regular engines and its hyperspace matrix. OPPOSITE: The energized plasma created by the ion scoops is channeled through a central exhaust and several smaller vector exhausts. The ship's wings, though small, are important to its operation in planetary atmospheres, as seen here over London.

DESCRIPTION AND OPERATIONAL HISTORY

The Guardians of the Galaxy go through spaceships the way the Avengers go through Quinjets. Their most recent ship is also nameless, with the Guardians presumably waiting for Rocket Raccoon to come up with a suitably witty moniker. Previous Guardians ships have been large enough to accommodate hundreds of people—and heavily armed enough to face down swarms of enemy spacecraft.

The ship is an arrowhead-shaped craft, with wide wings and a split tail indicating it is designed for both deep-space use and operation in planetary atmospheres. Additional stabilizer wings angle out from the bottom of the rear thruster housings, increasing atmospheric maneuverability. These retract for ground landings in the event that the ship must be powered down; otherwise it remains in a low hover, powered by secondary exhaust ports near the base of the retractable wings.

The ship is powered by six engines, two of which are modified tachyon/anti-tachyon reaction chambers designed to provide maximum physical thrust and warp capability. When the warp drive kicks in, the ship is able to traverse galactic distances more or less immediately with the aid of a semi-sentient navigational computer containing a galactic map updated continuously in real time. The reaction chambers also power the ship's internal gravitation field and outer energy shields.

(cont. on p. 110)

GUARDIANS OF THE GALAXY SHIP

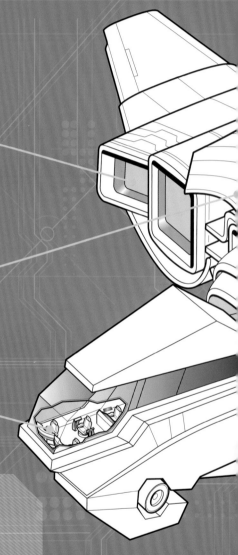

ION SCREENS PURIFY INTAKE FOR
FUEL REACTION IN EACH ENGINE

VARIOUS STABILIZERS ENABLE
ATMOSPHERIC OPERATION

HAWKSBILL BRIDGE DESIGN PUTS PILOT
AND CO-PILOT IN BEST POSITION TO
INCREASE FIELD OF VISION

GUARDIANS SHIP SPECS & FEATURES

CREW CAPACITY	12, even if one of them is Groot
PROPULSION	Eight engines fed by ionized plasma; two outside wing engines also able to generate thrust in hyperspace
WEAPONRY	Light combat energy weapons; fusion mines; anti-ship missiles; plasma cannons
AI CONTROL	Automated area multiple-target acquisition; course charting, docking, planetary landing
COCKPIT	Detaches to become flight-capable escape vehicle if ship is destroyed

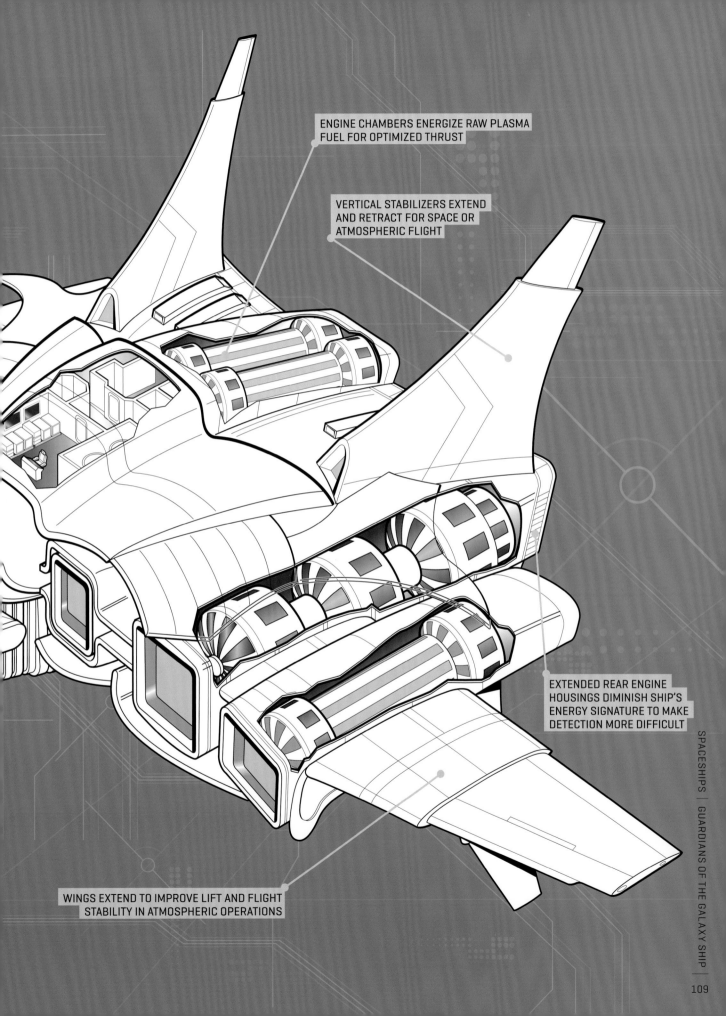

ENGINE CHAMBERS ENERGIZE RAW PLASMA
FUEL FOR OPTIMIZED THRUST

VERTICAL STABILIZERS EXTEND
AND RETRACT FOR SPACE OR
ATMOSPHERIC FLIGHT

EXTENDED REAR ENGINE
HOUSINGS DIMINISH SHIP'S
ENERGY SIGNATURE TO MAKE
DETECTION MORE DIFFICULT

WINGS EXTEND TO IMPROVE LIFT AND FLIGHT
STABILITY IN ATMOSPHERIC OPERATIONS

Integrated into the ship's navigational system is a full-spectrum surveillance and target-acquisition package that performs threat assessments on nearby vehicles. It is able to detect the energy signatures of most known weapons and automatically engages evasive maneuvers if the ship comes under attack when the pilot's chair is vacant. This system can also hack and access nearby satellites and other broadcast media, giving the Guardians close-range visual surveillance of any location in the view of a vulnerable camera.

The ship has no turret-mounted weaponry or visible hardpoints. Its weapons are contained in recessed hull mounts and include wingtip plasma cannons, chute-deployed fusion mines housed under the rear tail mounts, and batteries of anti-ship missiles in launch racks mounted internally along the sides of the nose. The cockpit area is able to separate from the rest of the ship and serve as an escape craft, utilizing its own power source for limited shielding, propulsion, and life support.

A workshop located in the rear of the craft has everything the Guardians need to repair, recharge, and upgrade their weapons and armor—or anyone else's, as Tony Stark found out when the Guardians pieced together the remains of a destroyed Iron Man suit. Living quarters are compact and utilitarian, suitable for the long-term

BELOW: The crew and passenger living area is not high end, but it does feature gravity generators set into the floor.
OPPOSITE: The ship's design, incorporating multiple directional thrusters and both vertical and horizontal stabilizers, is calibrated for both deep-space and atmospheric flight. Weapons systems are housed inside the hull, for better flight stability and less chance of damage by space debris.

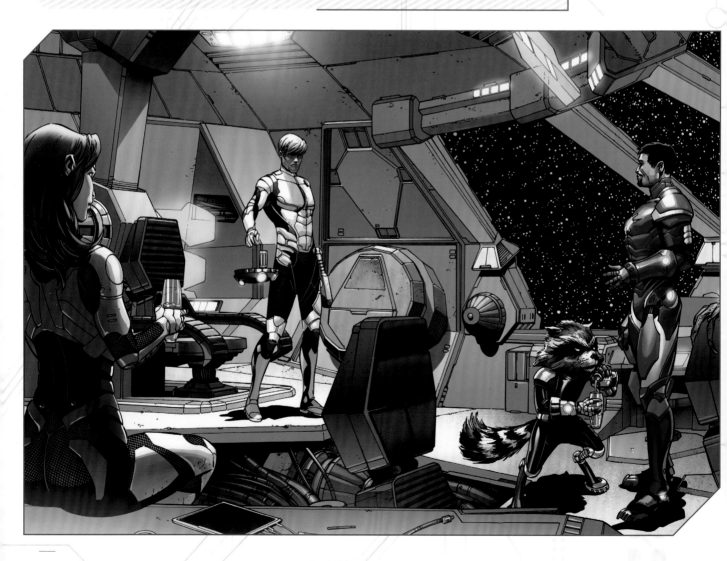

occupancy of as many as a dozen people. Some spaces are customized for the particular needs of individual Guardians, notably Groot. Onboard ship computers optimize the climate and atmospheric mix in each room, although the default settings for the common spaces are Earthlike.

There are four airlocks on the ship: one on each side where the wings meet the hull, one set in the underside of the nose below the bridge, and another below the common areas. This last airlock also has an extendable ramp for loading and unloading of cargo, and gives access to the ship's limited hold space.

ROCKET RACCOON

"I'VE FLOWN A LOT OF DIFFERENT SHIPS. IF IT'S GOT THRUSTERS, I CAN MAKE IT GO. BUT THIS ONE I LIKE MORE THAN MOST. FOR ONE THING, IT'S NOT THE SIZE OF A MOONLET. FOR ANOTHER, IT'S DESIGNED WITH ACTUAL PILOTING IN MIND, UNLIKE ANYTHING I'VE FLOWN SINCE THE DEAR DEPARTED RAKK 'N' RUIN. ONE OF THESE DAYS I'M GONNA BUILD ME ANOTHER ONE OF THOSE. BUT UNTIL THEN, I'LL FLY THIS ONE AND LOVE IT. WHEN YOU CAN GO FROM STATIONARY TO THE OTHER SIDE OF THE MAGELLANIC CLOUDS IN THE TIME IT TAKES TO BUCKLE YOUR SEAT HARNESS, THAT'S THE KIND OF PERFORMANCE A GUY LIKE ME CAN'T GET ENOUGH OF. PLUS IT'S GOT SOME GOODIES WE HAVEN'T SHOWN ANYONE YET. WHEN YOUR PRIMARY LEISURE ACTIVITY IS FIGHTING INTERSTELLAR THREATS, YOU HAVE TO KEEP SOME SECRETS."

FREEDOM'S LADY

GUARDIANS, WE'VE GOT *TROUBLE!* EVERYONE TO THE *BRIDGE!*

YONDU, BRING THE STARK WOMAN!

FREEDOM'S LADY SPECS & FEATURES

- **CREW CAPACITY** 2,058
- **DIMENSIONS** Length 1,850 feet; mass approximately 61,000 tons
- **PROPULSION** Tachyon drive, both normal- and hyper-space capable
- **WEAPONRY** Energy batteries, heavy anti-ship missiles designed for deep-space combat
- **AI CONTROL** Annihilator-class AI capable of multiple-target assessment and engagement, life support, automatic defense systems management

ABOVE: The design of Freedom's Lady—with its propulsion system mounted below the main hull—is geared toward deep-space operations.
OPPOSITE: The spoke-and-ring design of Drydock allowed for natural gravity in the outer ring while maintaining zero-gravity repair facilities in the central axis hull.

An Annihilator-class battlecruiser from the thirty-first century, Freedom's Lady was powered by a tachyon drive, giving it faster-than-light speed. It also carried heavy weapons capable of taking on other capital starships. Designed for deep-space operations, it was the Guardians' home until it was destroyed by the Stark. The Stark were a race of alien conquerors whose primitive society went through rapid advancement following the discovery of a cache of Tony Stark–created technology on their world.

DRYDOCK

DRYDOCK SPECS & FEATURES

- **ORIGIN** Badoon
- **DIMENSIONS** Unknown; central ring approximately 2.9 miles in diameter
- **FACILITIES** Complete life-support and living facilities for thousands of humanoid life-forms
- **SHIPYARD** 60 full-service docking, repair, reconstruction, and retrofitting bays
- **STATUS** Destroyed in Earth orbit, present day

This massive space station and shipyard originated in the thirty-first century and was a drifting hulk when the Guardians of the Galaxy discovered it in the aftermath of their war against the Badoon. A centralized artificial intelligence controlled the station's main functions, including life support and maintenance. It was heavily shielded against meteoroids and contained a fully operational starship construction facility as well as space for a crew of several thousand. It traveled by means of a warp drive, experimental even in the distant future. The Guardians of the Galaxy commandeered Drydock and used it as their traveling home base until they were catapulted back through time and the space station was destroyed by Korvac while in Earth orbit.

STAR-LORD (PETER QUILL)

RAKK 'N' RUIN

Rakk 'N' Ruin was Rocket Raccoon's original ship before he joined the Guardians. It was a small craft with a crew of only Rocket and his co-pilot Wal. Rocket flew Rakk 'N' Ruin while he served as a Ranger on Halfworld. A classic conical design with small stabilizers for atmospheric operation, Rakk 'N' Ruin took off and landed vertically. It was defended by powerful shields and featured a sophisticated package of surveillance and detection instruments necessary for Rocket's work as a Ranger. It was destroyed before he joined the Guardians.

"BEFORE I BECAME STAR-LORD, SHIP WAS MY FATHER'S FRIEND AND HOME AMONG THE STARS. ONCE SHE WAS A SENTIENT STAR, DESTROYED IN AN INTERSTELLAR WAR AND LEFT AS A DISEMBODIED CONSCIOUSNESS UNTIL THE MASTER OF THE SUN GUIDED HER IN CREATING HER FORM AS SHIP. SHE AND MY FATHER, J'SON OF SPARTAX, FOUGHT COSMIC ENEMIES, INCLUDING THE KREE, BEFORE HE CRASHED ON EARTH . . . AND THAT WAS HOW HE MET MY MOTHER AND THINGS GOT COOKING. ONE THING LED TO ANOTHER, YOU KNOW? EVENTUALLY I BECAME STAR-LORD LIKE MY FATHER BEFORE ME, AND SHIP PASSED TO ME AS WELL. SHE'S GOT IT ALL: GUNS, FASTER-THAN-LIGHT TRAVEL, FOOD AND WATER SYNTHESIZERS . . . AND LOYALTY. SHE'S SAVED MY LIFE MORE TIMES THAN I CAN COUNT, ONCE BY CREATING A HUMAN FORM TO NURSE ME WHEN I WAS BADLY WOUNDED IN A BATTLE WITH LORQ WARRIORS. I FELL IN LOVE WITH HER THEN, BUT SHE DOESN'T KEEP ONE FORM FOR LONG. IT'S A LOVE STORY BETWEEN ME AND HER, BUT MAYBE NOT ONE WITH A HAPPY ENDING. I LOST HER IN A BLACK HOLE YEARS AGO NOW, BUT I'LL FIND HER AGAIN. SHE KNOWS I'LL FIND HER. NOTHING IN THE WORLD MATTERS MORE. SO, I TAKE IT BACK. THERE WILL BE A HAPPY ENDING. COUNT ON IT."

--AND BOTH OF 'EM ARE CHASING US 'ROUND AND 'ROUND!

ICARUS

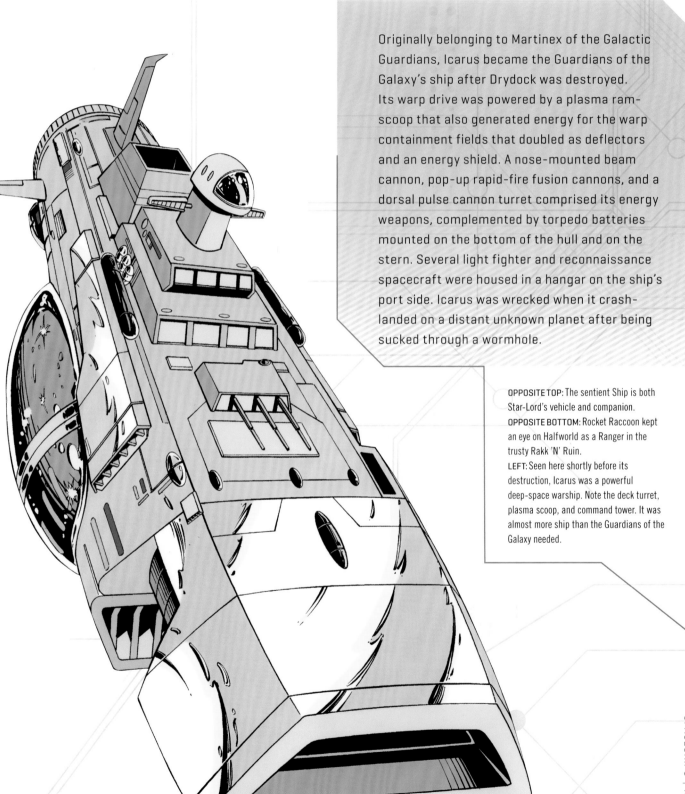

Originally belonging to Martinex of the Galactic Guardians, Icarus became the Guardians of the Galaxy's ship after Drydock was destroyed. Its warp drive was powered by a plasma ram-scoop that also generated energy for the warp containment fields that doubled as deflectors and an energy shield. A nose-mounted beam cannon, pop-up rapid-fire fusion cannons, and a dorsal pulse cannon turret comprised its energy weapons, complemented by torpedo batteries mounted on the bottom of the hull and on the stern. Several light fighter and reconnaissance spacecraft were housed in a hangar on the ship's port side. Icarus was wrecked when it crash-landed on a distant unknown planet after being sucked through a wormhole.

OPPOSITE TOP: The sentient Ship is both Star-Lord's vehicle and companion.
OPPOSITE BOTTOM: Rocket Raccoon kept an eye on Halfworld as a Ranger in the trusty Rakk 'N' Ruin.
LEFT: Seen here shortly before its destruction, Icarus was a powerful deep-space warship. Note the deck turret, plasma scoop, and command tower. It was almost more ship than the Guardians of the Galaxy needed.

ICARUS
"PRIDE OF MARTINEX"

PRIMARY RAMSCOOP POWERS BOTH THE
MAIN ENGINES AND THE WARP CONTAINMENT FIELD

HULL IS HEAVILY ARMORED AND DESIGNED TO
DISTRIBUTE ENERGY IMPACTS TO MINIMIZE DAMAGE

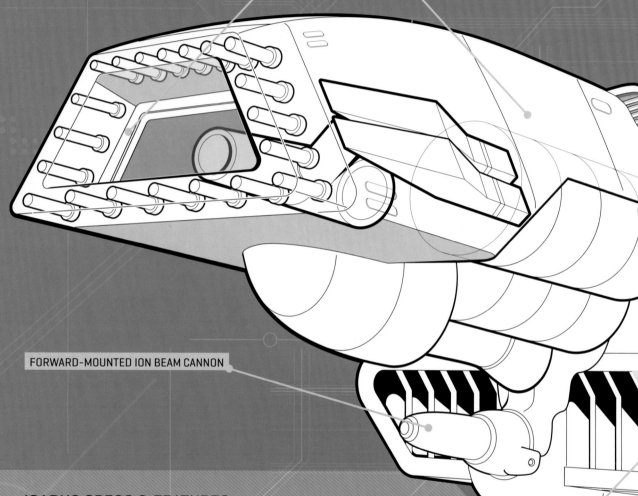

FORWARD-MOUNTED ION BEAM CANNON

MIDDLE LEVELS CONTAIN
CREW QUARTERS, MEDICAL
AND SCIENCE FACILITIES

ICARUS SPECS & FEATURES

CREW CAPACITY	4,000; minimum 3
DIMENSIONS	Length 940 feet; mass 68,000 tons
PROPULSION	Plasma ramscoop; also power source for warp drive
DEFENSE SYSTEMS	Energy-dampening shields capable of absorbing incoming energy discharges and routing them to onboard reservoirs
WEAPONRY	Fusion, ion beam, laser pulse cannon turrets; automatically targeted torpedo batteries
HANGAR	As many as 24 light fighter and reconnaissance spacecraft, most capable of automated operation under control of shipboard AI

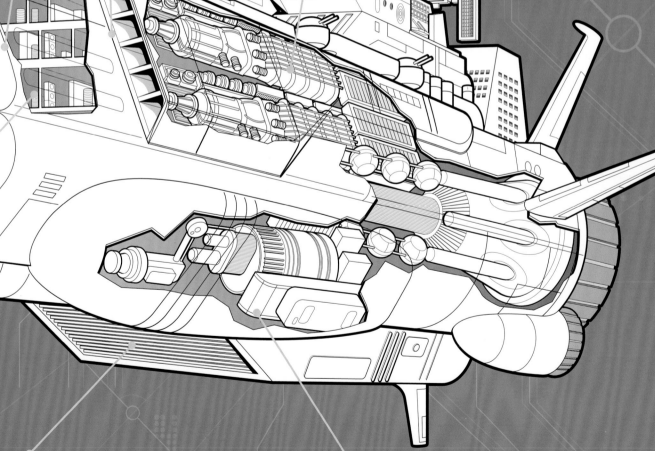

CENTRAL PORTION OF SHIP
DEDICATED TO LIVING QUARTERS
AND MAINTENANCE FACILITIES

WARP CONTAINMENT FIELD POWERED BY
ANTIMATTER HARVESTED FROM RAMSCOOP INTAKE

CONTROL TOWER HOUSES COMMAND STAFF
AND COMBAT OBSERVATION/TARGETING AI

SIDE-HULL PARTICLE INTAKES
CONTRIBUTE TO ENERGY RESERVOIRS

RETRACTABLE GRILL COVERING
SMALL CRAFT HANGARS

LOWER LEVELS OF HULL CONTAIN FUSION MINE
DISCHARGE TUBES AND OTHER DEFENSE SYSTEMS

SKUTTLEBUTT

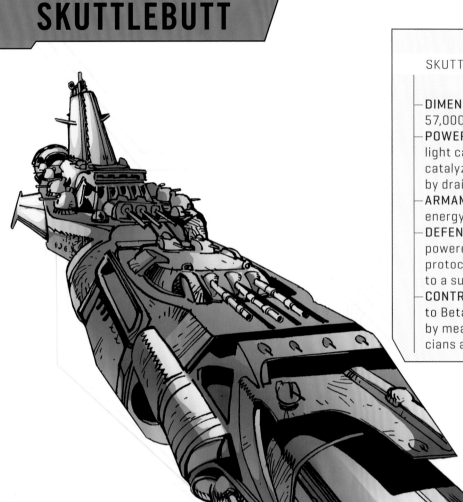

SKUTTLEBUTT SPECS & FEATURES

- **DIMENSIONS** Length 549 feet; mass 57,000 tons
- **POWER AND PROPULSION** Faster-than-light capable, using Korbinite ion-catalyzed star drive; energy replenished by draining stars
- **ARMAMENTS** Turret-mounted and fixed energy cannons; fusion mines
- **DEFENSE SYSTEMS** Energy shielding powered by star drive; self-destruct protocol with energy release equivalent to a supernova
- **CONTROL SYSTEMS** Fully sentient, loyal to Beta Ray Bill; capable of self-repair by means of onboard robotic technicians as well as nanotech replicators

LEFT: Skuttlebutt's lines and turrets recall the famous designs of twentieth-century fleet battleships.

OPPOSITE: Starjammer's enormous size makes it an odd choice for a pirate crew, but there are few ships that can match its firepower.

BETA RAY BILL

"THE OL' GAL, I LIKE TO CALL HER. SHE'S SAVED MY LIFE MORE TIMES THAN I CAN COUNT, AND KEPT THE KORBINITES FROM TOTAL EXTINCTION. SKUTTLEBUTT AND I WERE CREATED AT AROUND THE SAME TIME, FOR THE SAME REASON: TO PROTECT KORBIN. WE COULDN'T DO THAT. SURTUR AND HIS LEGIONS DESTROYED OUR GALAXY, PRETTY MUCH, BEFORE I COULD STOP HIM. BUT SKUTTLEBUTT AND I, WE'VE DONE SOME GOOD IN THE UNIVERSE. WE FOUGHT OFF OTHER THREATS, FROM GALACTUS AND HIS HERALDS TO SOME OF EARTH'S HEROES WHO HAD THE WRONG IDEA UNTIL THEY GOT TO KNOW US. SHE'S GOT A DOZEN CANNONS HEAVY ENOUGH TO VAPORIZE A STARSHIP AND A SELF-DESTRUCT MECHANISM THAT COULD ANNIHILATE EVERYTHING WITHIN A LIGHT-YEAR. SHE'S ALSO GOT MINES AND ENERGY SHIELDS. ALL THOSE WEAPONS TAKE A LOT OF ENERGY, AND SHE REFUELS ONCE IN A WHILE BY DRAINING THE ENERGY OF A STAR.

THERE AREN'T TOO MANY SHIPS OUT THERE LIKE HER. AND THAT'S BEFORE WE TALK ABOUT HOW SHE'S SENTIENT AND ABLE TO COMPLETELY SELF-REPAIR. I'VE SEEN HER SHOT ALL TO PIECES AND GOOD AS NEW A WEEK LATER. DON'T KNOW WHAT I'D DO WITHOUT HER."

STARJAMMER

POLARIS

STARJAMMER SPECS & FEATURES

- **DIMENSIONS** Overall length 201,755 feet; main hull 21,950 feet; mass approximately 1.2 billion tons
- **POWER AND PROPULSION** Shi'ar Par-Meson Hyperlight Engine, maximum output 200 terajoules
- **ARMAMENTS** Twin dorsal particle-beam cannons; battery of eight particle-beam cannons mounted ventrally; 10-barrel particle-beam battery on a fixed mount near bridge
- **DEFENSE SYSTEMS** Active energy shielding automatically engaged when sensors detect targeting of ship
- **CONTROL SYSTEMS** Neural interface provides pilot with real-time command and control over all ship systems; individual subsystems can be delegated for outside control

"CHRISTOPHER SUMMERS TOLD ME ALL THE STORIES BEFORE HE WAS GONE. THE STARJAMMERS GOT TOGETHER AND BROKE OUT OF A SHI'AR LABOR CAMP, STEALING A SHIP ALONG THE WAY AND DECIDING TO BECOME PIRATES. CHRISTOPHER SUMMERS, RAZA, CH'OD, HEPZIBAH . . . THAT WAS BEFORE THEY GOT BACK TO EARTH AND CHRISTOPHER SAW WHAT HAD HAPPENED TO HIS BOYS SCOTT AND ALEX, ALL GROWN UP AS X-MEN. IT WAS ALSO BEFORE HIS THIRD SON, WHO WE ALL THOUGHT WAS DEAD, SHOWED UP AND TRIED TO TAKE OVER THE SHI'AR EMPIRE. WE STOPPED HIM, BUT CHRISTOPHER DIDN'T MAKE IT. SOME OF THE TEAM LEFT THEN, BUT HAVOK–ALEX–DECIDED TO STICK AROUND. I DECIDED TO STAY WITH HIM. HE WAS TRYING TO LIVE UP TO HIS FATHER'S EXAMPLE. BELIEVE ME, I KNOW HOW HARD THAT CAN BE. NEITHER OF US STAYED WITH THE STARJAMMERS, BUT WE HAD SOME TIMES. WE FOUGHT SKRULLS, SHI'AR, THE COLLECTOR . . . AT SOME POINT WE STOPPED BEING PIRATES AND TURNED OURSELVES INTO HEROES. I'M NOT SURE WHEN THAT HAPPENED, BUT ONE THING I AM SURE OF: WE'D ALL HAVE BEEN DEAD WITHOUT THAT SHIP."

ABOVE: It is unknown if the structure of Taa II is just a design feature or reflects a warping of physical space inside the ship.

TAA II SPECS & FEATURES

DIMENSIONS	Not precisely known; length would be measured in hundreds of millions of miles; mass is sufficient to exert gravitational influence on nearby planetary bodies and stars
WEAPONS	Elemental Converter, able to drain and store the latent energies of planetary ecosystems by means of extruded tendrils inserted into planetary crust
MENAGERIE	Part of the ship's interior is divided into thousands of pocket environments for housing life forms captured for study over millions of years
WORLDSHIP	Hull constructed in the shape of a Möbius strip; materials taken from the remains of Archeopia, first planet consumed by Galactus in this universe

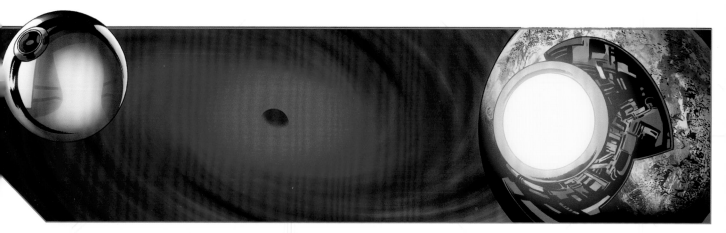

TOP: The Star Sphere is vast and formidable.
ABOVE: Galactus is seen here focusing the Elemental Converter.

STAR SPHERE SPECS & FEATURES

- **DIMENSIONS** Planet-scale size and mass; varies with activities of Elemental Converter
- **WEAPONS** Elemental Converter (see Taa II, opposite page)
- **DEFENSE SYSTEMS** Punisher robots deploy upon unauthorized entry or at Galactus' command
- **CONTROL SYSTEMS** Navigational systems contain complete model of known universe; control and guidance systems partly overseen by captured consciousnesses of sentient beings
- **OTHER FEATURES** Regeneration chamber assists healing of Galactus or other beings, tapping reservoir of energy created by Elemental Converter

HANK PYM

"TAA II, THE WORLDSHIP, IS THE CLOSEST THING GALACTUS HAS TO A HOME. IT'S BUILT ON A PLANETARY SCALE AND DWARFS MOST PLANETS. GALACTUS BUILT IT FROM THE REMAINS OF THE FIRST PLANET HE EVER CONSUMED, AND NAMED IT IN HONOR OF HIS OWN HOME WORLD, TAA, A PARADISE THAT EXISTED PRIOR TO THE BIG BANG THAT CREATED OUR UNIVERSE. TAA II TAKES THE SHAPE OF AN INFINITY SYMBOL, WITH SHARP ANGLES INSTEAD OF THE ELLIPTICAL CURVES NORMALLY CHARACTERISTIC OF THAT PATTERN. I BELIEVE THIS IS AN INTENTIONAL PIECE OF DESIGN ON GALACTUS' PART, TO REFLECT HIS OWN BELIEF THAT HE IS ESSENTIALLY INFINITE.

GALACTUS ALSO USES A SMALLER—BUT STILL GIGANTIC—SHIP KNOWN AS THE STAR SPHERE TO MOVE AMONG WORLDS. THE STAR SPHERE IS EQUIPPED WITH EXTENDABLE TENDRILS USED TO DRILL INTO PLANETARY BODIES AND ACCELERATE THE EXTRACTION OF THEIR BIOSPHERIC ENERGIES FOR GALACTUS' CONSUMPTION. LIKE TAA II, IT CAN BE SUMMONED FROM ANYWHERE IN THE UNIVERSE WHENEVER GALACTUS NEEDS IT; AND LIKE TAA II, ITS TECHNOLOGY IS SO ADVANCED THAT MUCH OF IT IS INCOMPREHENSIBLE, EVEN TO ME."

CARS & VANS

THE PUNISHER'S BATTLE VAN

ABOVE: The Battle Van's armor can handle not just bullets, but most handheld energy weapons as well.

DESCRIPTION AND OPERATIONAL HISTORY

As part of his pitiless war on crime, the Punisher had his partner, the Mechanic, design the very first Battle Van. Built on a standard passenger-van chassis, the Battle Van had a turbocharged V-8 engine rated for 270 horsepower, four-wheel drive, enhanced suspension and control mechanisms for pursuit and combat driving, and an armored exterior that shrugged off small-arms fire. Solid rubber tires kept the van moving through any terrain and combat environment. The stiffness of the tires was compensated by a set of hydraulic equalizers built into the driver's seat, keeping the driver stable even when the Battle Van was bouncing over uneven surfaces. The windows were double-layered throughout and enhanced with transparent composites in the front windows and windshield.

The Battle Van's armaments included a retractable turret-mounted minigun chambered for the .223 round and a 40mm grenade launcher. The minigun could also switch to nonlethal ammunition on command. As different missions demanded different tactics and ordnance, the Punisher and his allies constantly added to the Battle Van's arsenal, notably upgrading to sonic weaponry when the Punisher clashed with Venom. One of the van's side doors was designed to open and rotate out to provide a protected firing platform, usable either at rest or while the van was in motion. The interior was a mobile command center and weapons locker, carrying every imaginable variety of weapon.

After the Mechanic was killed, the Punisher partnered up with Linus Lieberman, the hacker and engineer known as Microchip. New versions of the Battle Van were based on updated SUV-style frames instead of the classic van. They carried advanced electronic upgrades, including an artificial intelligence that allowed the van to operate under remote command. This system can follow simple commands, enabling the Punisher to use the van as a decoy or carry out unmanned ramming attacks. Sophisticated onboard computer systems can monitor communications across CB, police,

[cont. on p. 128]

THE PUNISHER

"A GUY LIKE ME DOESN'T HAVE A HOME. HE HAS A BASE. AND THE BEST BASES ARE MOBILE, SO THE ENEMY NEVER KNOWS WHERE YOU'LL BE NEXT. EVERYTHING I NEED IS IN THE VAN . . . EXCEPT TARGETS. I CAN FIND THOSE ANYWHERE. IN THE VAN, I CAN SEE EVERYTHING THAT HAPPENS AROUND ME, IN ANY PART OF THE ELECTROMAGNETIC SPECTRUM FROM INFRARED RIGHT UP TO MICROWAVE. I CAN HACK COMPUTERS ON THE OTHER SIDE OF THE PLANET. I CAN DRIVE THROUGH BRICK WALLS LIKE THEY'RE BANKS OF FOG. IT'S GOT EVERY WEAPON I CAN THINK OF ON BOARD, AND THAT MEANS EVERY WEAPON THERE IS. IF IT CAN INCAPACITATE OR KILL A MAN, I'VE GOT IT IN THE VAN. I ALWAYS DID LIKE TO DRIVE. NOW I CAN DRIVE AND FIGHT AT THE SAME TIME.

THE WAR IS FOREVER. THE SCUM OUT THERE IS ALWAYS LOOKING FOR BETTER TOOLS, BETTER WEAPONS, BETTER INTEL. THAT MEANS I HAVE TO LOOK HARDER. EVERY TIME THEY FIGURE OUT SOMETHING NEW, I HAVE TO BE THERE AHEAD OF THEM. FAILURE IS NOT AN OPTION—IT'S NOT EVEN SOMETHING YOU CONSIDER AS A POSSIBILITY. YOU CAN'T WIN A WAR BY THINKING OF THE WAYS YOU MIGHT NOT WIN. YOU WIN IT BY DOING EVERYTHING YOU CAN BETTER THAN THE OTHER GUY . . . STARTING WITH WEAPONS AND SECURITY. AND THAT STARTS WITH THE VAN."

LEFT: The Battle Van is a weapon, a mobile HQ, and command center. It also sometimes doubles as an infirmary and DIY surgical center.

THE PUNISHER'S BATTLE VAN

MODEL 2011-X, "BESTRAFE"

RADAR AND INFRARED DETECTION SYSTEMS; SATELLITE UPLINK; REMOTE-ACCESS SENSOR SUITE

ROOF PLATFORM WITH DEPLOYABLE ROCKET LAUNCHER

BELT-FED .50 CALIBER GATLING GUN

ROLL BAR ALSO LOCKS DOWN IN A FORWARD POSITION FOR RAMMING

3.7-LITER TURBOCHARGED INLINE-5 ENGINE

DRIVER'S SEAT COMPENSATES FOR SUDDEN MOVEMENTS AND DRIVING OVER BROKEN TERRAIN

WINDSHIELD HOLOGRAPHICALLY INTEGRATED WITH COMMUNICATIONS AND SURVEILLANCE SYSTEMS

BATTLE VAN SPECS & FEATURES

ENGINE	3.7-liter, inline-5, turbocharged, max horsepower 312
WEAPONS SYSTEMS	Multiple small-caliber, single-barrel and Gatling cannons; energy discharges from hubcaps; side-facing flamethrowers mounted under chassis; systems automatically interlock fields of fire and assign individual targeting responsibilities
DEFENSE SYSTEMS	Anti-theft protocols prevent ignition by unauthorized persons; exterior electrified when Punisher is not present; passenger-side Gatling cannon targets thieves and vandals
STEERING AND CONTROL	Heads-up displays give 360-degree view with automatic targeting in combat situations
OTHER FEATURES	Mobile medical unit for treatment of battlefield injuries; satellite uplink using anonymized access technologies; remote access permits steering and fire control from up to one mile away

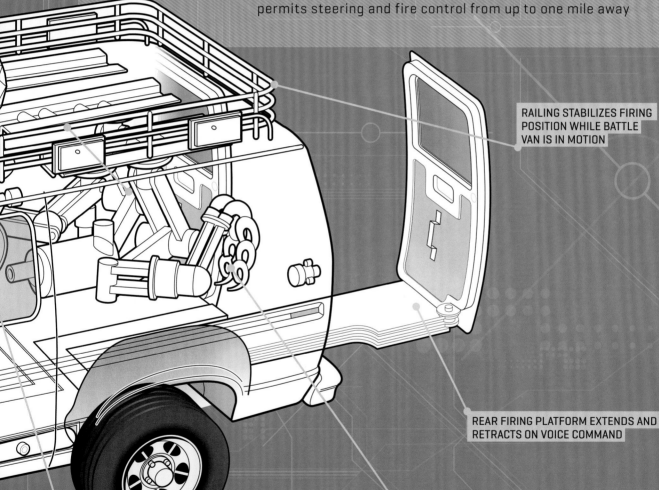

RAILING STABILIZES FIRING POSITION WHILE BATTLE VAN IS IN MOTION

REAR FIRING PLATFORM EXTENDS AND RETRACTS ON VOICE COMMAND

MULTIPLE HEAVY WEAPONS ON FLEX-CONTROL ARMS

ONE-WAY BULLETPROOF GLASS, TRIPLE-LAYERED

SPIDER-MAN

"I'M THE ONLY GUY I KNOW WHO'S EVER SNUCK INTO THE BATTLE VAN . . . BUT THAT WAS A LONG TIME AGO. NO WAY I'D TRY IT NOW. FRANK AND I, WE GET ALONG OKAY, BUT YOU MIGHT SAY HE'S THE KIND OF GUY WHO VALUES HIS SECURITY OVER HIS FRIENDS. IF HE HAS ANY FRIENDS."

fire department, and a number of other frequencies, including satellite signals. It can be used to remotely hack computer systems as well. Active sonar and thermal imaging sensors detect targets and coordinate with fire-control software that can deploy the minigun and grenade launcher even when the Punisher is not in the van. This software also links to the Battle Van's nonlethal combat systems, including tear gas and smoke dispersal, rubber bullet guns, and a man-trap arm assembly that extends from the rear of the van. A winch mounted on the underside of the frame is rated to 15 tons.

From the driver's seat, the Punisher can observe the immediate area using infrared and night-vision equipment. Directional microphones capture and enhance sound for surveillance operations. The Battle Van's security systems include anti-personnel shaped charges, a pain-field emitter, plasma projectors housed behind the hubcaps, and software protocols that prevent the vehicle from being used by anybody but Frank Castle.

In the event of a rollover, the Punisher can exit the van using either the escape hatch built into the floor or explosive bolts that can remove damaged doors. If the van is submerged, an emergency air supply activates, giving ample time to don the wetsuit and emergency breathing apparatus stored in a locker across from the weapons racks. Gas-deployed parachutes are available in the event of the Battle Van falling from a non-survivable height.

THE PUNISHER'S MOTORCYCLE

OPPOSITE: With the battle van on autopilot, the Punisher starts to deploy the rear firing platform.

ABOVE: For missions where speed and maneuverability are more important than armored firepower, the Punisher maintains a custom motorcycle.

For moving quickly—and when he doesn't think he'll need the resources of the Battle Van—the Punisher also keeps a motorcycle fueled up and ready to go at all times. It's a custom job, built to his exact specifications, right down to the death's-head image on the fairing.

HOBGOBLIN'S BATTLE VAN

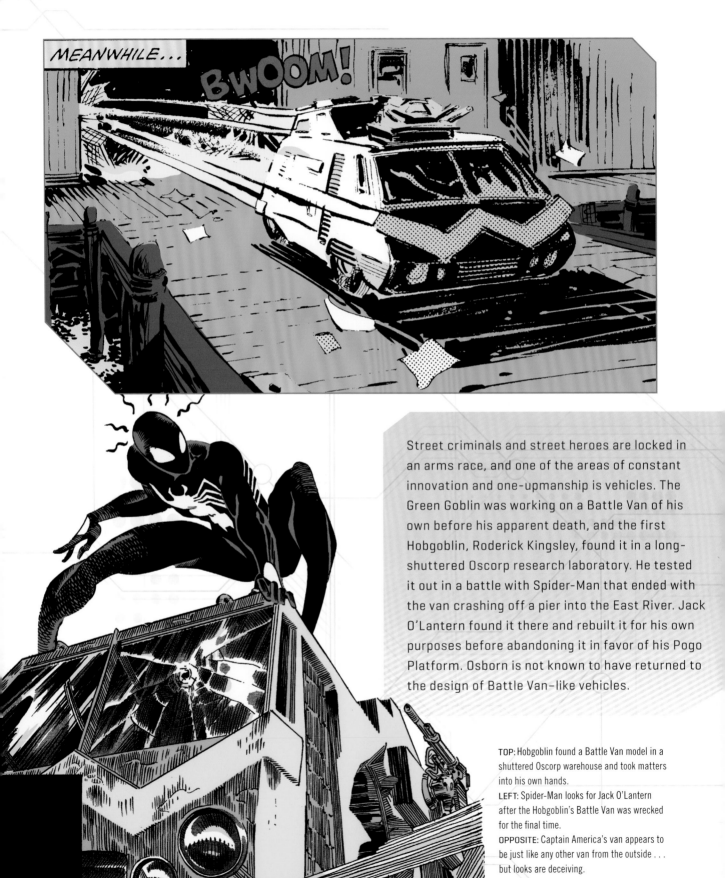

Street criminals and street heroes are locked in an arms race, and one of the areas of constant innovation and one-upmanship is vehicles. The Green Goblin was working on a Battle Van of his own before his apparent death, and the first Hobgoblin, Roderick Kingsley, found it in a long-shuttered Oscorp research laboratory. He tested it out in a battle with Spider-Man that ended with the van crashing off a pier into the East River. Jack O'Lantern found it there and rebuilt it for his own purposes before abandoning it in favor of his Pogo Platform. Osborn is not known to have returned to the design of Battle Van–like vehicles.

TOP: Hobgoblin found a Battle Van model in a shuttered Oscorp warehouse and took matters into his own hands.

LEFT: Spider-Man looks for Jack O'Lantern after the Hobgoblin's Battle Van was wrecked for the final time.

OPPOSITE: Captain America's van appears to be just like any other van from the outside . . . but looks are deceiving.

CAPTAIN AMERICA'S VAN

CAPTAIN AMERICA

"YOU CAN'T RIDE INTO EVERY BATTLE IN A QUINJET OR ON A SKY-CYCLE. SOMETIMES YOU NEED TO TAKE ANOTHER APPROACH. WHEN I NEED TO DO SURVEILLANCE ON A SUSPECTED ENEMY HIDEOUT, OR WHEN I'M TRAVELING ON A MISSION WITHOUT WANTING TO CALL ATTENTION TO MYSELF, I USE THE VAN. BLACK PANTHER'S WAKANDA DESIGN GROUP BUILT IT FOR ME. IT'S GOT EVERYTHING I NEED. THERE'S A COT IN THE BACK FOR A QUICK FORTY WINKS, A STAND FOR MY MOTORCYCLE, AND A SATELLITE UPLINK TO THE HELICARRIER. SUSPENSION IS UPGRADED AND THE WHOLE EXTERIOR, INCLUDING THE GLASS, IS BULLETPROOF. THAT'S COME IN HANDY. THE VAN NEVER DRAWS ATTENTION TO ITSELF, EITHER. I CAN SWITCH LICENSE PLATES WITH A BUTTON ON THE DASHBOARD,

AND THE BRAINIACS IN WAKANDA ALSO CAME UP WITH AN ADVANCED EXTERIOR FINISH THAT CHANGES TO ANY COLOR OR PATTERN I CHOOSE FROM A PRESET MENU. I CAN ALSO CUSTOMIZE THAT FINISH BY FOCUSING ONE OF THE VAN'S CAMERAS ON ANOTHER VEHICLE AND COMMANDING THE COMPUTER TO MIMIC ITS LOOK.

IT'S BEEN UPGRADED A FEW TIMES SINCE THE FIRST MODEL. NOW IT'S GOT GPS, SMART GLASS DISPLAYS, AND A REMOTE NAVIGATION SYSTEM THAT LETS ME DRIVE IT UNMANNED FROM ANY LOCATION. THAT COMES IN HANDY WHEN I WRECK THE BIKE, WHICH HAS HAPPENED MORE THAN ONCE.

HE WOULD NEVER ADMIT IT, BUT I'M BETTING THE PUNISHER IS JEALOUS."

SPIDER-MOBILE

ABOVE: The Spider-Mobile's debut did not achieve the effect its designers might have hoped for.

OPPOSITE: Existing in a distant future, this version of the Spider-Mobile is redesigned for desert all-terrain operation, and features a strengthened frame.

The Spider-Mobile came about when a bunch of automotive marketing executives decided, for reasons known only to themselves, that Spider-Man would be an ideal spokesman for a new zero-emission engine they had prototyped. The company offered Spidey an endorsement deal with one simple catch: They would provide the engine, but the construction of the rest of the car was up to him. Needing the cash, Spidey agreed, and with a little help—make that a lot of help, since this was before he developed his engineering and science skills beyond web-shooters—the Spider-Mobile was built.

The Spider-Mobile was built on a heavy off-road frame and suspension, but with aerodynamic lines that gave the vehicle the look of a dune buggy. Heavy roll bars protected the driver in the event of a rollover accident. The tires were wide, with heavy tread, offering all-terrain stability. Each hubcap was an enameled reproduction of Spider-Man's mask. The Spider-Mobile's bugeye headlights folded down to make way for twin forward-mounted automatic web-shooters, which were activated and fired from a dashboard switch. Another switch lit up the Spider-Signal projector, aimed by a joystick and with a focused range of more than one hundred yards. The seat was equipped with an ejector mechanism.

Spider-Man took his new wheels out for their first test drive without benefit of driving lessons. As a native New Yorker, he'd never bothered to learn—although the Spider-Mobile did have a custom SPIDEY license plate. After some on-the-fly instruction, he started to get the

[cont. on p. 137]

SPIDER-MAN

" I SHOULD HAVE KNOWN BETTER. MARKETING GUYS COME UP WITH DUMB IDEAS ALL THE TIME, AND USUALLY I HAVE ENOUGH SPIDEY-SENSE TO STEER CLEAR. THIS TIME, THOUGH, I NEEDED THE MOOLAH, AND HEY, WHO DOESN'T LOVE A COOL CAR? I'M NOT GOING TO LIE TO YOU, I HAD A BLAST ZOOMING AROUND NEW YORK. I WAS EVEN STARTING TO GET THE HANG OF PARALLEL PARKING. BUT EASY COME, EASY GO. I'M JUST GLAD I DIDN'T GET TURNED INTO A TRAFFIC STATISTIC WHEN THE TINKERER HAD HIS FUN. ONE OF THESE DAYS I'M REALLY GOING TO HAVE TO GET A DRIVER'S LICENSE. "

SPIDER-MOBILE
CORONA MOTORS CM-S1 "ARACHNE"

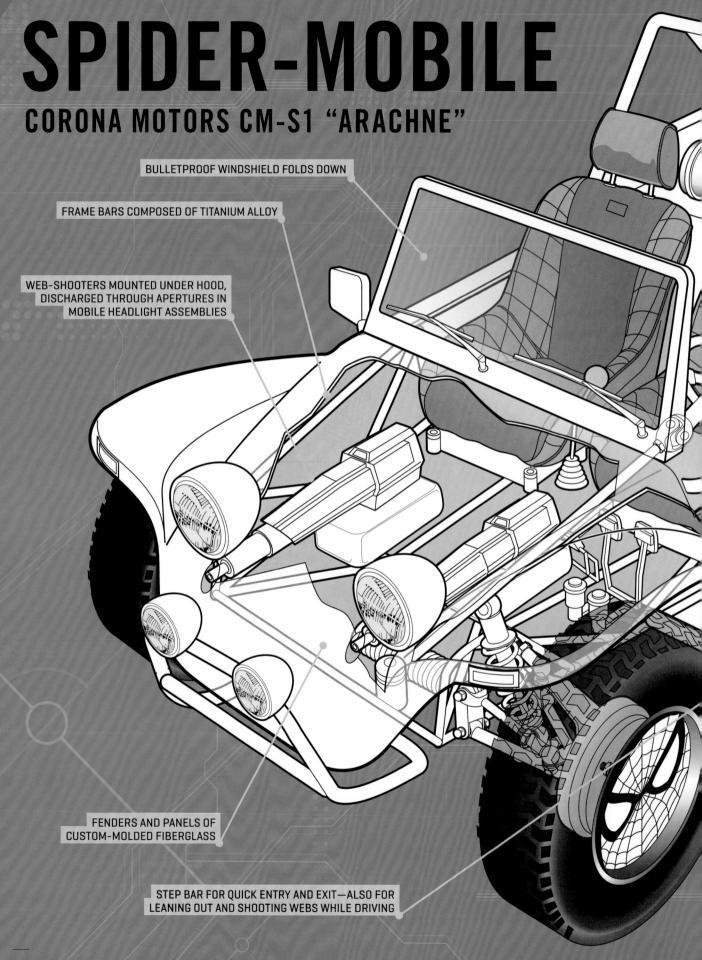

BULLETPROOF WINDSHIELD FOLDS DOWN

FRAME BARS COMPOSED OF TITANIUM ALLOY

WEB-SHOOTERS MOUNTED UNDER HOOD,
DISCHARGED THROUGH APERTURES IN
MOBILE HEADLIGHT ASSEMBLIES

FENDERS AND PANELS OF
CUSTOM-MOLDED FIBERGLASS

STEP BAR FOR QUICK ENTRY AND EXIT—ALSO FOR
LEANING OUT AND SHOOTING WEBS WHILE DRIVING

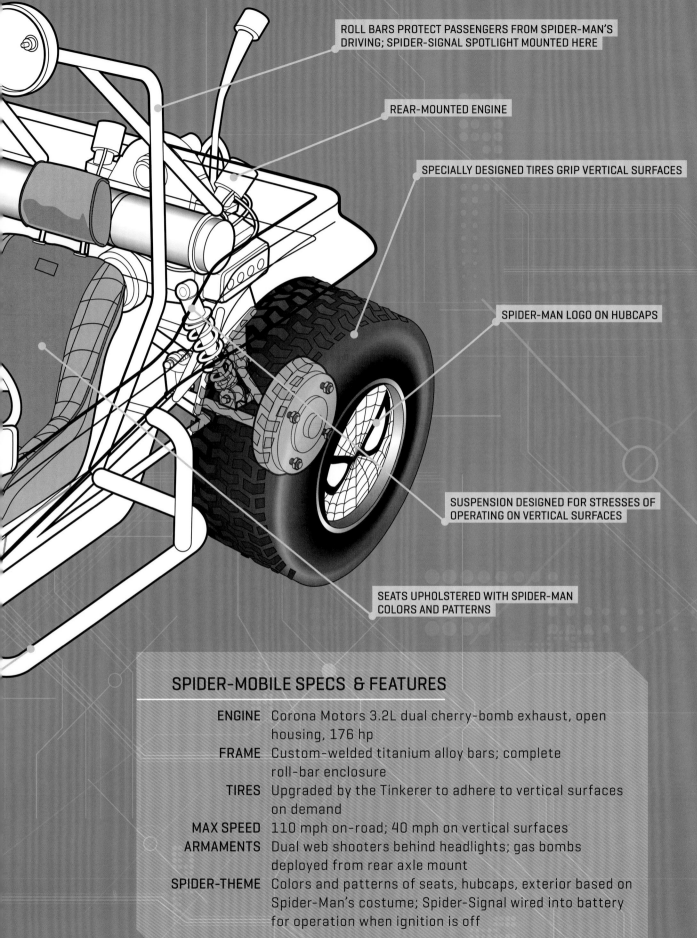

ROLL BARS PROTECT PASSENGERS FROM SPIDER-MAN'S
DRIVING; SPIDER-SIGNAL SPOTLIGHT MOUNTED HERE

REAR-MOUNTED ENGINE

SPECIALLY DESIGNED TIRES GRIP VERTICAL SURFACES

SPIDER-MAN LOGO ON HUBCAPS

SUSPENSION DESIGNED FOR STRESSES OF
OPERATING ON VERTICAL SURFACES

SEATS UPHOLSTERED WITH SPIDER-MAN
COLORS AND PATTERNS

SPIDER-MOBILE SPECS & FEATURES

ENGINE	Corona Motors 3.2L dual cherry-bomb exhaust, open housing, 176 hp
FRAME	Custom-welded titanium alloy bars; complete roll-bar enclosure
TIRES	Upgraded by the Tinkerer to adhere to vertical surfaces on demand
MAX SPEED	110 mph on-road; 40 mph on vertical surfaces
ARMAMENTS	Dual web shooters behind headlights; gas bombs deployed from rear axle mount
SPIDER-THEME	Colors and patterns of seats, hubcaps, exterior based on Spider-Man's costume; Spider-Signal wired into battery for operation when ignition is off

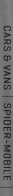

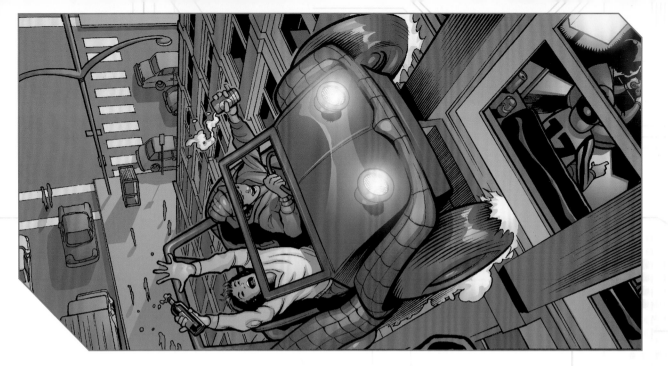

ABOVE: The Tinkerer's souped-up version of the Spider-Mobile had ultra-grip tires that let it climb vertical surfaces.

RIGHT: A closeup of the web projectors in operation, with the headlight assemblies folding down so as not to obstruct firing.

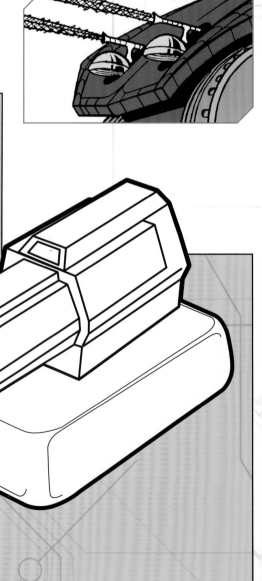

HOOD-MOUNTED WEB-SHOOTER SPECS & FEATURES

CONTROL	Fired from steering wheel button; when pressed, button folds down headlights to clear firing aperture
HOUSING	Mounted to crossbar parallel to front axle, under hood
TANK	5 gallon capacity
BARREL	30 inches long, 1-inch diameter; self-cleaning between discharges to prevent clogging
RANGE	Stream effective to 200 feet; less in high winds

hang of it, and immediately ran the Spider-Mobile into a heist planned by Hammerhead's goons. Shortly thereafter an illusion created by Mysterio tricked Spider-Man into driving the Spider-Mobile off a pier, where he escaped without benefit of the ejector seat. Ready to give up on his driving adventures, Spider-Man left the Spider-Mobile at the bottom of the Hudson River, but his enemy the Tinkerer raised it, repaired it, and added new features. These included special gripping tires, a gravity localizer that decreased the vehicle's mass without affecting its angular momentum, and an electron gyroscope designed to keep the vehicle operational on vertical surfaces. Its original power train was also replaced with a much more powerful engine that made it possible to jump the Spider-Mobile across the gaps between Manhattan buildings.

With the Spider-Mobile under remote control, the Tinkerer used the car to attack Spider-Man, putting its new all-surface abilities to use before trapping Spidey with the vehicle's web shooters. Taken to the Tinkerer's laboratory, Spider-Man escaped, and in the ensuing fight the Spider-Mobile was critically damaged. Swearing off driving for good, Spider-Man left the Spider-Mobile hanging outside the offices of the advertising agency that came up with the gimmick in the first place.

ABOVE: Once he got the Spider-Mobile on the streets, Spider-Man found himself regretting that he'd never learned to drive.

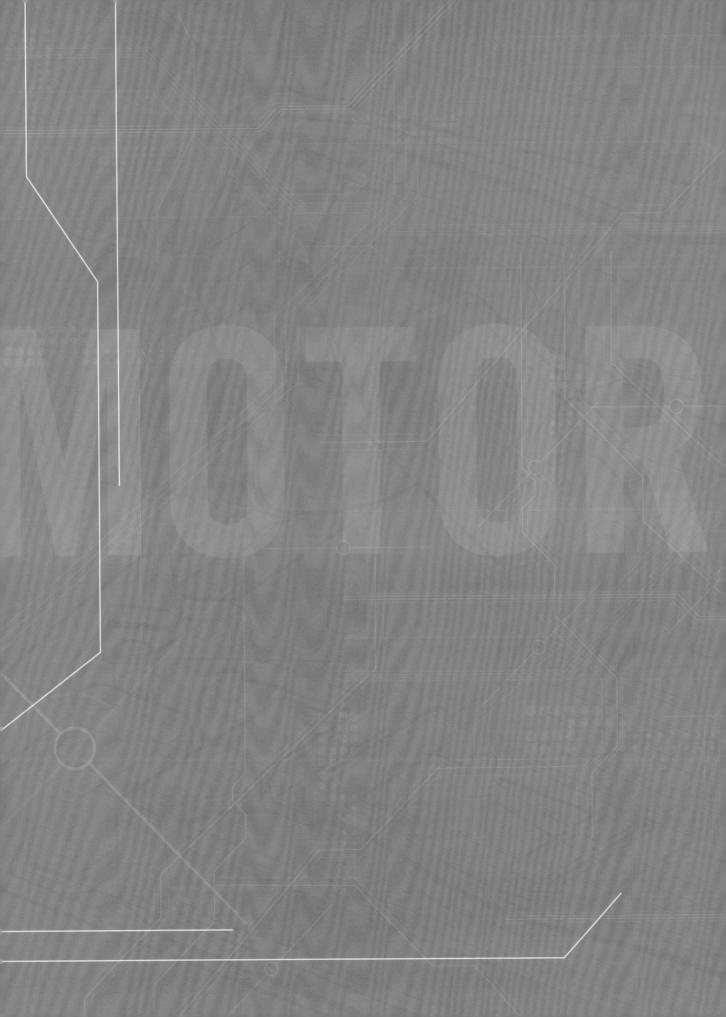

MOTORCYCLES

GHOST RIDER'S HELLCYCLE

ABOVE: Throughout history, Ghost Riders have needed something to ride—most of them have come to prefer motorcycles.
OPPOSITE: Where Ghost Rider goes, hellfire goes too . . . but his better nature is never completely lost.

DESCRIPTION AND OPERATIONAL HISTORY

Created by Mephisto for his Spirits of Vengeance, the Hellcycle is a supernatural mode of transport that takes the form of a motorcycle. Whoever rides the Hellcycle is known as Ghost Rider, although the name is most often associated with Johnny Blaze. The Hellcycle can travel faster than any other wheeled vehicle, and is capable of climbing vertical surfaces, crossing bodies of water, and even short periods of flight. At times Ghost Rider is even able to ride it from Earth to Hell and back. The Hellcycle is under the Ghost Rider's command even when he is not riding it. He can call the Hellcycle to him at any time and command it remotely. [cont. on p. 145]

HELLCYCLE

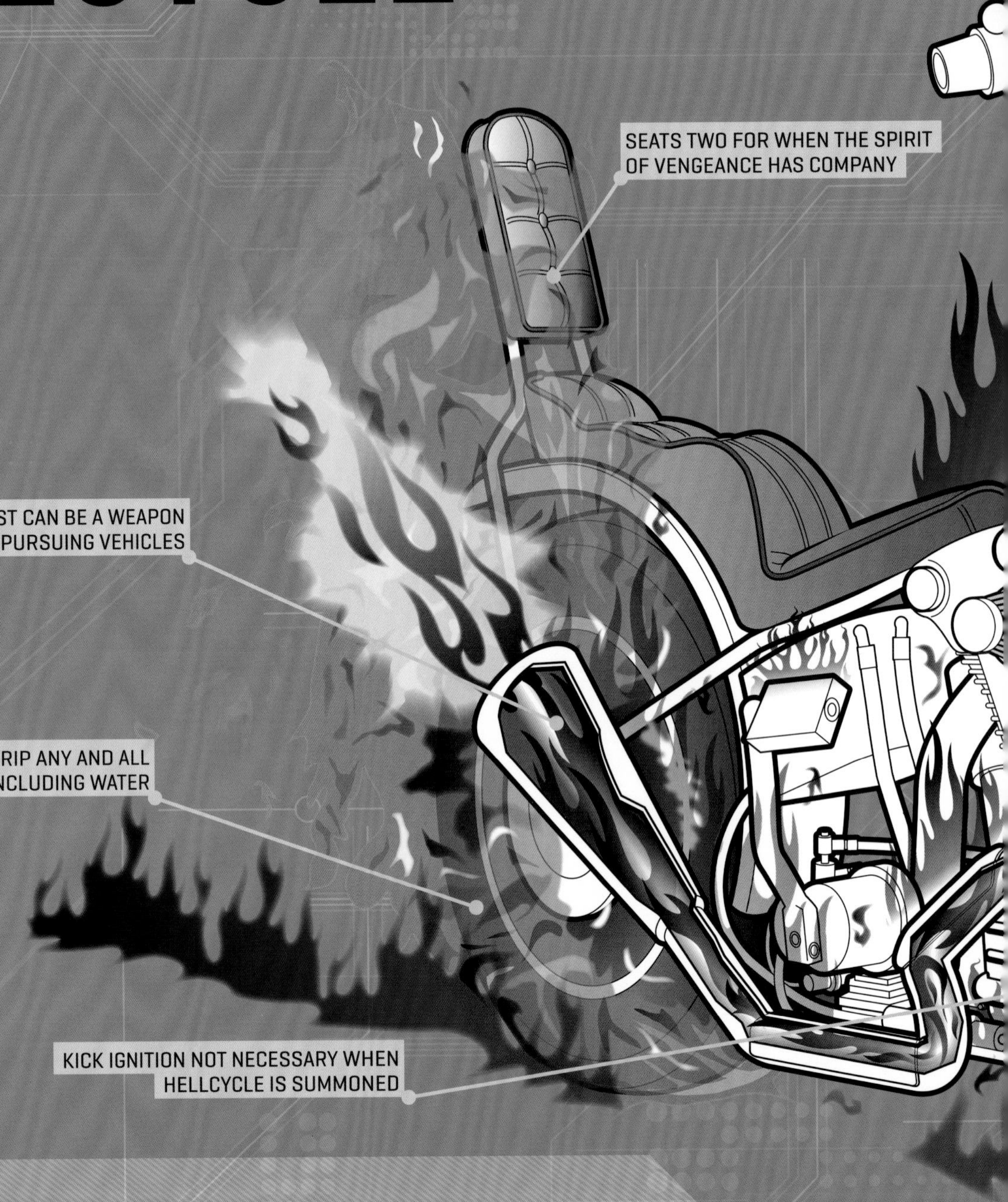

SEATS TWO FOR WHEN THE SPIRIT
OF VENGEANCE HAS COMPANY

HELLFIRE EXHAUST CAN BE A WEAPON
AGAINST PURSUING VEHICLES

TIRES GRIP ANY AND ALL
SURFACES, INCLUDING WATER

KICK IGNITION NOT NECESSARY WHEN
HELLCYCLE IS SUMMONED

HELLCYCLE SPECS & FEATURES

MODEL Varies

ENGINE Varies with model

MAX SPEED Uncertain, but Ghost Rider has been observed to travel
across the United States in a matter of hours

RANGE Unlimited

OTHER FEATURES Hellcycle is able to travel from Earth to Hell, but not
always back, depending on Mephisto's will; leaves a
trail of fire even over water

BRAKING CAUSES REACTION BETWEEN HELLFIRE AND SURFACE, OFTEN MELTING ROADWAY

HEADLIGHT POWERED BY HELLFIRE; OTHER MODELS DISPLACE HEADLIGHTS FOR SKULL-SHAPED AILERON

HELLFIRE SPILL CAN IGNITE NEARBY OBJECTS BUT DOES NOT CONSUME TIRES

GAS TANK CONTAINS INEXHAUSTIBLE SUPPLY OF HELLFIRE

ABOVE: An older version of the Hellcycle that is just as deadly for any criminal gangs who get in Ghost Rider's way. RIGHT: The Hellcycle carries no standard onboard weapons, but it is a powerful weapon itself . . . as Ghost Rider's enemies often find out.

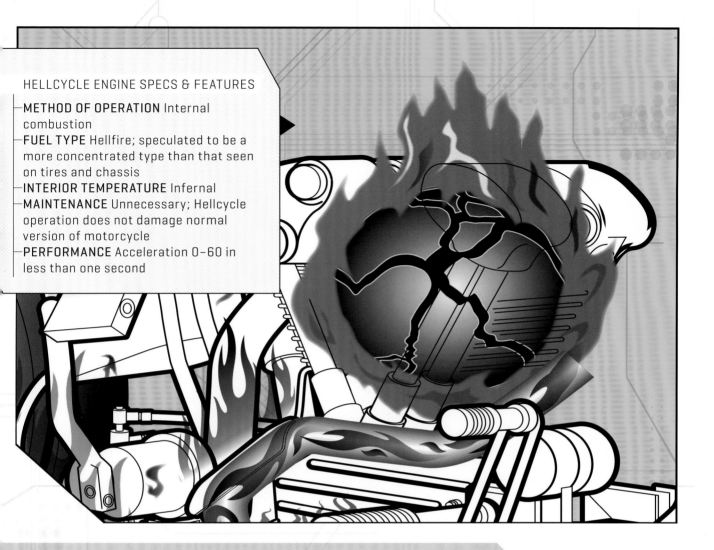

HELLCYCLE ENGINE SPECS & FEATURES

- **METHOD OF OPERATION** Internal combustion
- **FUEL TYPE** Hellfire; speculated to be a more concentrated type than that seen on tires and chassis
- **INTERIOR TEMPERATURE** Infernal
- **MAINTENANCE** Unnecessary; Hellcycle operation does not damage normal version of motorcycle
- **PERFORMANCE** Acceleration 0–60 in less than one second

Due to the Hellcycle's supernatural nature, the details of its workings remain mysterious, and the assessment here must be considered highly speculative. Hellcycles can be created from any model of motorcycle, and have been observed being brought into existence solely through Ghost Rider's Hellfire abilities. The transformation of the motorcycle by demonic power means it no longer runs on gasoline, but instead is powered by pure hellfire.

The composition of the tires is transformed from high-performance synthetic rubber to an inexhaustible semi-solid form of hellfire, although this has not been established with any authority. These wheels burn constantly, causing the Hellcycle to leave a trail of fire wherever it goes; this fire is also a powerful weapon, as a number of Ghost Rider's enemies have discovered. The rest of the Hellcycle also spits hellfire, particularly the exhaust, as if some demonic form of internal combustion occurs within the transformed engine. If this is the case, the internal process that drives the Hellcycle either does not consume hellfire or taps into an inexhaustible supply. Since the Spirits of Vengeance are infused with hellfire themselves, it is possible that Hellcycles are powered by a limitless fuel supply sourced from the infernal realms.

DAN KETCH'S HELLCYCLE

ABOVE: Hellfire burns a different color for Dan Ketch. Note the skull-shaped aileron, which can be both a shield and a weapon.

When Dan Ketch was Ghost Rider, his motorcycle featured the Medallion of Power in the form of the vehicle's gas cap. Before he fully understood his abilities, Ketch needed to touch the Medallion to become Ghost Rider, but later he learned to undertake the transformation at will. Ketch's Hellcycle could be reformed if destroyed using his powers as the Spirit of Vengeance. It departed in design particulars from Johnny Blaze's original Hellcycle, featuring a fairing in the shape of an armored mask rather than the skull that was standard for Blaze's Hellcycle. This fairing could also be lowered and used as a battering ram.

NOBLE KALE'S HELLCYCLE

The Spirit of Vengeance that was bonded to Dan Ketch was revealed to be Noble Kale, the first Ghost Rider, who was part of a bargain between Mephisto and Noble's warlock father in the eighteenth century. After Noble Kale's amnesia was lifted and he realized the truth of his origins, he separated from Ketch and assumed his own corporeal form. He also created his own motorcycle, composed of pure hellfire. This marked a change in the nature of the Hellcycle, as the individual Spirits of Vengeance learned more about the nature and use of their powers and no longer needed to use the template of a physical motorcycle.

Hellcycles created from Hellfire display little in the way of mechanical origin, as early models of the cycle did. They still take the basic shape of motorcycles, but where early models maintained a metallic chassis, newer versions solidify Hellfire itself by means of a mystical process understood only by the Spirits of Vengeance—and, presumably, their demonic creators.

LEFT: When Hellfire dissipates, a Ghost Rider's motorcycle looks like an ordinary machine.

VENGEANCE'S HELLCYCLE

Michael Badilino sold his soul to Mephisto in return for the power to destroy the demon Zarathos, whom he blamed for destroying his family. Believing Daniel Ketch to be Zarathos in disguise, he tried to kill Ketch but later learned the truth about the demon's nature—and about his own destiny as the latest incarnation of the Spirit of Vengeance. His version of the Hellcycle was designed with chrome elements recalling the skull and ribs of a dragon, but its power source, as with all Hellcycles, was pure hellfire.

RIGHT: Vengeance's cycle, a Hellfire-breathing, skeletal chrome dragon on wheels.

ROBBIE REYES' STREET ROD

STREET ROD SPECS & FEATURES

SOURCE MODEL	Unknown; early-70s vintage likely
ENGINE	5.7L supercharged V8; details unknown due to Hellfire
MAX SPEED	Unknown
FEATURES	Hellfire spill from grille evokes appearance of demonic eyes; Hellfire blazes from hood scoop under certain circumstances; possible the car itself is the host of the Spirit of Vengeance

ABOVE: Robbie Reyes' street rod was fast even before the Spirit of Vengeance gave it the kind of turbo boost only Hellfire can deliver.

The Spirit of Vengeance has made the move from two wheels to four. Looking to escape his crime-plagued Los Angeles neighborhood and protect his wheelchair-bound kid brother Gabe, young mechanic Robbie Reyes entered a street race with a purse of fifty thousand dollars. His car? A custom street rod he "borrowed" from the shop where he worked.

The race was broken up by a group of men in a helicopter who appeared to be the police, but once they isolated Robbie they shot him dead and removed a bag of contraband from the car. At that moment the Spirit of Vengeance reached out and reanimated Robbie, while transforming his car into a Hellfire vehicle. The car was already a unique item, with everything from the tires to the exhaust meticulously upgraded with aftermarket parts—most of which Robbie had installed himself. Its top speed before the Spirit of Vengeance emerged was close to 200 miles per hour on a good road, as a result of its 5.7-liter supercharged V8 kicking out 400-plus horsepower. Now, with Hellfire replacing horsepower, it can comfortably exceed that, and the car has added powers akin to the Hellcycles.

SKY-CYCLE

ABOVE: Although the Sky-Cycle is identified with Hawkeye, the other Avengers have had their own variations, too.

OPPOSITE: Sky-Cycles have autopilot features for hands-free operation, but it also works to have someone else fly while you shoot.

DESCRIPTION AND OPERATIONAL HISTORY

The first Sky-Cycle was created for Hawkeye by Jorge Latham at Cross Technological Enterprises. It was powered by a high-yield turbine with air intake through a vent in the nose below the handlebar assembly. Thrust angle and lift were controlled by secondary turbines with adjustable vents on the bottom of the frame under the driver's seat. Maximum speed at sea level was 380 miles per hour, with a rate of climb approximating 800 feet per second and a flight ceiling of 12,000 feet. The vehicle could be piloted with the handlebars, but a primary feature of its design was hands-free operation so Hawkeye could fly and shoot at the same time. [cont. on p. 154]

SKY-CYCLE 1
1970S-ERA "SKY PILOT"

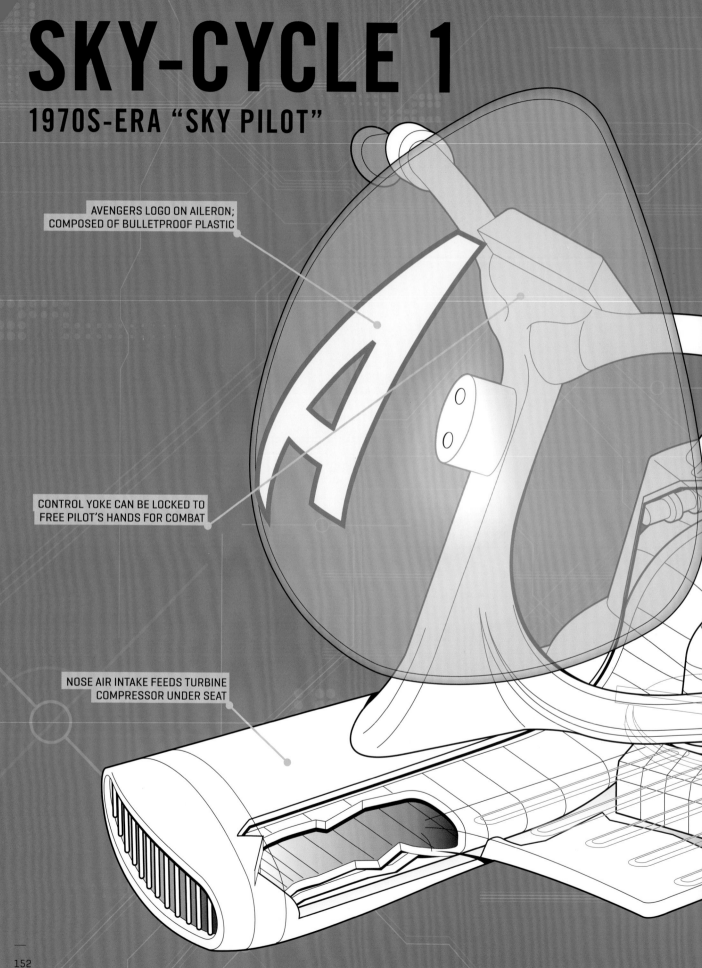

AVENGERS LOGO ON AILERON;
COMPOSED OF BULLETPROOF PLASTIC

CONTROL YOKE CAN BE LOCKED TO
FREE PILOT'S HANDS FOR COMBAT

NOSE AIR INTAKE FEEDS TURBINE
COMPRESSOR UNDER SEAT

CLASSIC SKY-CYCLE SPECS & FEATURES

CREW CAPACITY	2 people, up to 500 pounds max
WEIGHT	550 pounds
MAX SPEED	225 mph
MAX ALTITUDE	1,000 feet
RANGE	200 miles with two passengers
ENGINE	Stark Industries multi-intake turbine, variable exhaust
WEAPONS SYSTEMS	None
DEFENSIVE SYSTEMS	None

SEAT'S LOW PROFILE CLEARS THE WAY FOR THE PILOT TO SHOOT IN ANY DIRECTION WHILE FLYING

MAIN EXHAUST NOZZLE FOR FORWARD THRUST

SECONDARY EXHAUST NOZZLE GIVES VARIABLE THRUST TO ASSIST STEERING

FUEL TANKS ON EITHER SIDE OF VEHICLE WITH FEED LINE TO A MIXING CHAMBER BELOW TURBINE COMBUSTOR

VENTS ON BOTTOM OF FRAME CHANNEL EXHAUST FROM DEFLECTOR DUCTS FOR MANEUVERABILITY AND CUSHIONED LANDING

This was accomplished with an autopilot routine programmed for simple one-touch commands to hover, maintain speed, or respond to shifts in the pilot's weight. The Sky-Cycle was designed for a single operator but was powerful enough to carry a single passenger behind the operator. Because Hawkeye—and, later, several of the Sky-Cycle's other operators—cannot fly, the cycle came equipped with a parachute deployed by a switch on the main control console.

After the original was destroyed, Hawkeye commissioned more Sky-Cycles while he was leading the West Coast Avengers. Some of these were personalized with flight helmets and color schemes identified with Hawkeye. Later they became available to other Avengers as well, in a standardized design. Various different turbine models and configurations were also part of the development process.

As turbine technology was replaced in Avengers and S.H.I.E.L.D. vehicles by newer energy- and plasma-based systems, the Sky-Cycle too was updated. The enhanced model of the Sky-Cycle is powered by a compact ion engine that delivers greater thrust than the original turbine design. The new propulsion technology also makes more efficient use of deflector panels to channel thrust for change in direction and altitude. The lateral and ventral exhaust ports operate with less waste heat and less noise, providing stealth advantages as well as increased

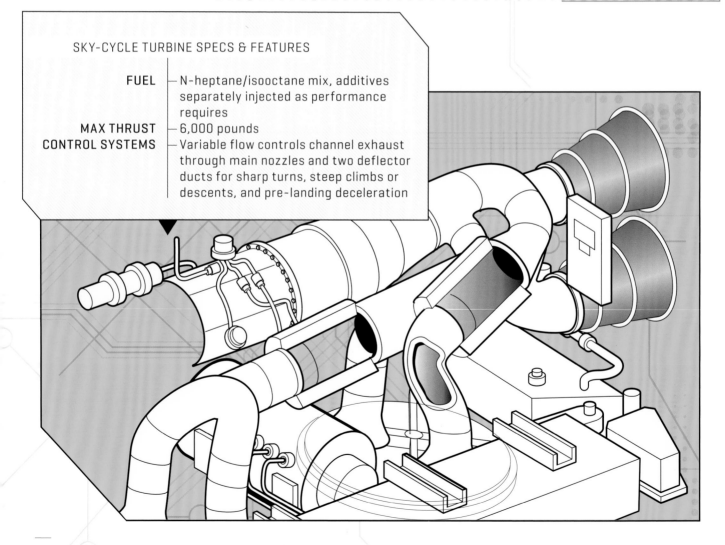

SKY-CYCLE TURBINE SPECS & FEATURES

FUEL	N-heptane/isooctane mix, additives separately injected as performance requires
MAX THRUST	6,000 pounds
CONTROL SYSTEMS	Variable flow controls channel exhaust through main nozzles and two deflector ducts for sharp turns, steep climbs or descents, and pre-landing deceleration

IF YOU SAY SO SPORT!

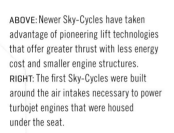

ABOVE: Newer Sky-Cycles have taken advantage of pioneering lift technologies that offer greater thrust with less energy cost and smaller engine structures.
RIGHT: The first Sky-Cycles were built around the air intakes necessary to power turbojet engines that were housed under the seat.

maneuverability. Voice command has replaced the pre-programmed flight options of the previous generations, and the autopilot functionality is much more robust.

Some versions of the Sky-Cycle have been designed to operate both on the ground and in the air, with functional wheels that shift and relock in a different configuration for flight. This design innovation results from a partnership between S.H.I.E.L.D. and the Avengers, deploying the tilt-wheel design and universal-joint axle pioneered in the early S.H.I.E.L.D. flying cars. The front wheel of this cycle is held in place by an electromagnetic field, powered by an arc reactor.

This frictionless assembly enables both incredible rotational velocity—and therefore ground speed—and the seamless transfer from ground-based to aerial operation. The arc reactor also functions with minimum shedding of heat, so

these new Sky-Cycles require much less shielding than previous versions. It is also programmed with sophisticated autopiloting software that tracks Hawkeye's location and returns the cycle to him if he is separated from it in mid-air. The autopilot has combat functionality as well, with threat assessment and target acquisition that enable it to become a 400-pound projectile that delivers quite a blow when traveling at high speed.

GENESIS COALITION VARIANT

The Genesis Coalition, a breakaway sect of Hydra, used a variation on the Sky-Cycle design during their actions against Silver Sable's Wild Pack. Notable similarities to the original Cross Enterprises design suggest that the Genesis Coalition either pirated that design or reverse-engineered their own Sky-Cycles from a unit abandoned by the Avengers.

SKY-CYCLE 2
2000S-ERA STARK TECH TR-CLASS

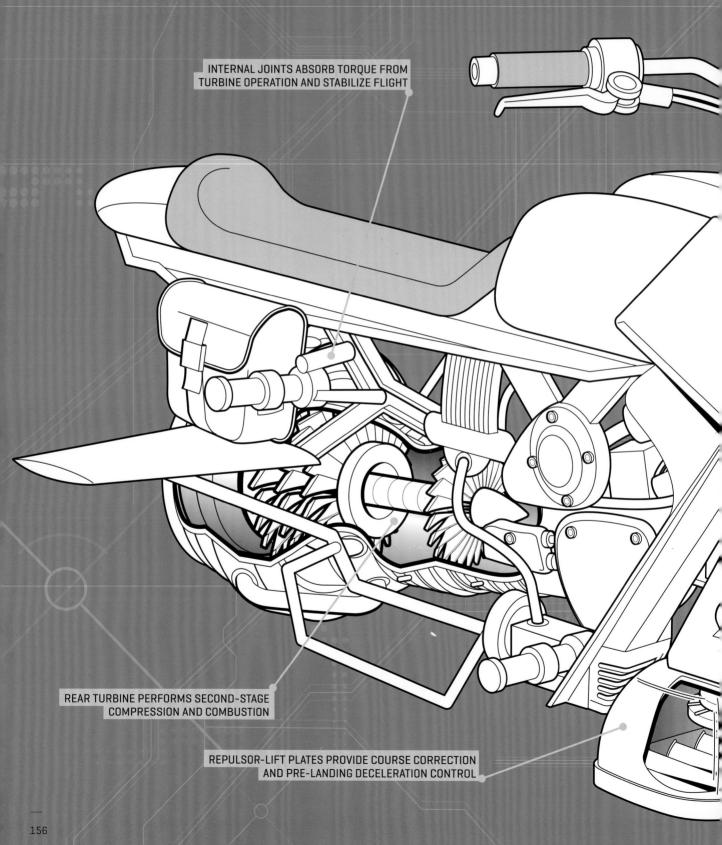

INTERNAL JOINTS ABSORB TORQUE FROM TURBINE OPERATION AND STABILIZE FLIGHT

REAR TURBINE PERFORMS SECOND-STAGE COMPRESSION AND COMBUSTION

REPULSOR-LIFT PLATES PROVIDE COURSE CORRECTION AND PRE-LANDING DECELERATION CONTROL

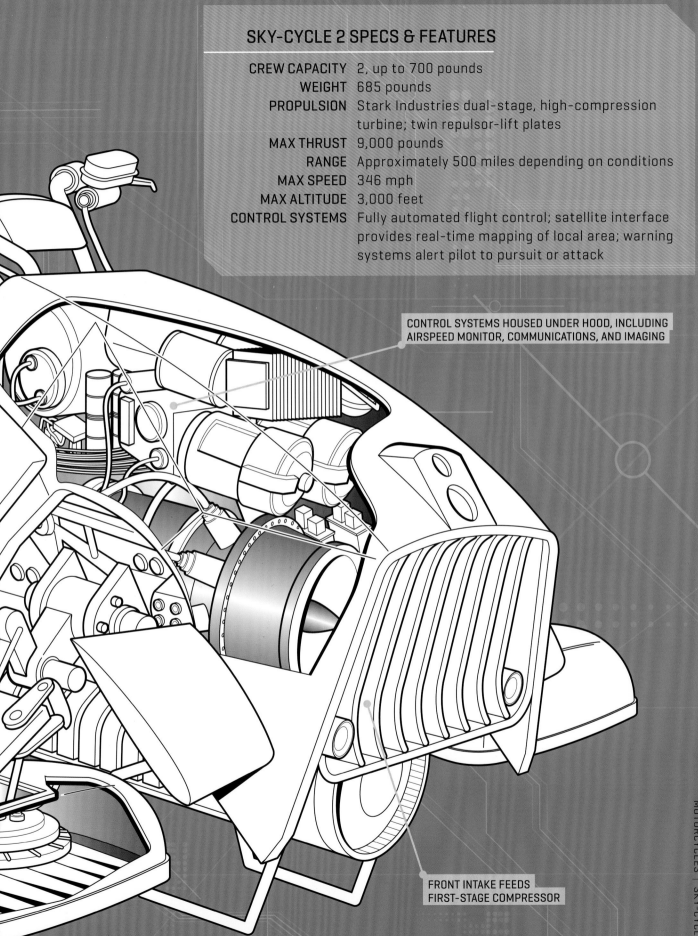

SKY-CYCLE 2 SPECS & FEATURES

CREW CAPACITY	2, up to 700 pounds
WEIGHT	685 pounds
PROPULSION	Stark Industries dual-stage, high-compression turbine; twin repulsor-lift plates
MAX THRUST	9,000 pounds
RANGE	Approximately 500 miles depending on conditions
MAX SPEED	346 mph
MAX ALTITUDE	3,000 feet
CONTROL SYSTEMS	Fully automated flight control; satellite interface provides real-time mapping of local area; warning systems alert pilot to pursuit or attack

CONTROL SYSTEMS HOUSED UNDER HOOD, INCLUDING AIRSPEED MONITOR, COMMUNICATIONS, AND IMAGING

FRONT INTAKE FEEDS FIRST-STAGE COMPRESSOR

CYCLOPS' MOTORCYCLE

CYCLE SPECS & FEATURES

- **TOP SPEED** 211 mph on-road, variable off-road
- **ENGINE** Worthington Industries RH04 771cc V-Twin, generating 204 horsepower
- **CUSTOM ENHANCEMENTS** Wireless communications linked to speakers in Cyclops' visor

CYCLOPS

" I'VE HAD A FEW BIKES OVER THE YEARS, AND LOVED ALL OF THEM. I DON'T SEEM TO BE ABLE TO HOLD ONTO ANY OF THEM, THOUGH. ONE TIME I WAS ON A SOLO ROAD TRIP TO ALASKA, JUST THINKING, TRYING TO GET MY HEAD TOGETHER AFTER XAVIER TOLD ME HE THOUGHT I NEEDED SOME TIME AWAY FROM THE X-MEN. THAT HAD WORKED ONCE BEFORE, AFTER JEAN DIED; I THOUGHT HE MIGHT BE RIGHT AGAIN. SO I HIT THE ROAD, AND THE FIRST THING THAT HAPPENS IS I RUN INTO JUGGERNAUT AND BLACK TOM CASSIDY, WORKING FOR SOMEONE I'D NEVER HEARD OF: ULYSSES. TO FIND OUT WHAT WAS GOING ON, I HAD TO DITCH MY BIKE AND STOW AWAY ON THEIR PLANE. SOMEONE'S PROBABLY STILL RIDING IT NOW. THAT WAS A NICE BIKE. "

CAPTAIN AMERICA'S MOTORCYCLE

CYCLE SPECS & FEATURES (MODEL AS SEEN)

TOP SPEED	197 mph
ENGINE	Stark Industries 837cc inline four, multivariable intake, generating 214 horsepower
EXHAUST	Stark Industries supercooling expansion chambers for minimal exhaust noise and vibration
AILERON	Specialized bracketing over front wheel for placement of Captain America's shield as protection or battering ram

OPPOSITE: This model of Cyclops' bike has a little extra ground clearance and slightly heavier tires for off-road use.
LEFT: As old-fashioned as he is, Captain America is in step with modern safety measures. When he rides, he usually wears a helmet.

CAPTAIN AMERICA

"BEFORE I HAD THE VAN, I HAD A BIKE. I'VE LOVED MOTORCYCLES SINCE I FIRST GOT TO DRIVE ONE DURING THE WAR. I USUALLY KEEP ONE IN THE VAN, BUT I ALSO HAVE A ROOFTOP STORAGE SPOT AT MY PLACE IN BROOKLYN WITH A BACKUP. I STICK TO HARLEYS BECAUSE THEY'RE AMERICAN-MADE. THE FIRST ONE WAS A CUSTOM SPECIAL WITH SOME ADDITIONS AND UPGRADES BY JONATHAN COULSON, A YOUNG MECHANIC GRATEFUL THAT I HELPED HIM BURY THE HATCHET WITH HIS FATHER. HE GAVE IT A PAINT JOB MATCHING MY COSTUME, TUNED UP THE PERFORMANCE, AND MADE IT A LITTLE QUIETER. WELL, A LOT QUIETER. EVEN WHEN I GOT IT WOUND UP OVER 100 MILES AN HOUR, IT DIDN'T SOUND MUCH LOUDER THAN A BLOW DRYER. THE NEW BIKE I KEEP ON THE ROOF IS FASTER AND SLICKER. I DON'T LIKE ANYONE ELSE RIDING IT, AND I STILL OWE FLASH THOMPSON A PUNCH IN THE JAW FOR THE TIME HE STOLE IT WHILE I WAS AT PROJECT REBIRTH."

This edition published by Haynes Publishing
Sparkford, Yeovil
Somerset BA22 7JJ, UK
Tel: 01963 442030 Fax: 01963 440001
Int. tel: +44 1963 442030
Int. fax: +44 1963 440001
E-mail: sales@haynes.co.uk
Website: www.haynes.co.uk

Published 2014 in the United States by Insight Editions, PO Box 3088, San Rafael, CA 94912

A catalogue record for this book is available from the British Library
ISBN 978 0 85733 792 4

Publisher: Raoul Goff
Acquisitions Manager: Robbie Schmidt
Executive Editor: Vanessa Lopez
Senior Editor: Chris Prince
Art Director: Chrissy Kwasnik
Designer: Chris Kosek
Production Editor: Rachel Anderson
Production Manager: Jane Chinn
Editorial Assistants: Elaine Ou & Kathryn DeSandro

Insight Editions would like to thank Chelsea Alon, Mark Annunziato, Curt Baker, Sarah Brunstad, Graham Cook, David Gabriel, Joseph Hochstein, Brian Overton, Steve Rendle, Danny Saeva, Iain Wakefield, and Jeff Youngquist.

ROOTS of PEACE   REPLANTED PAPER

Insight Editions, in association with Roots of Peace, will plant two trees for each tree used in the manufacturing of this book. Roots of Peace is an internationally renowned humanitarian organization dedicated to eradicating land mines worldwide and converting war-torn lands into productive farms and wildlife habitats. Roots of Peace will plant two million fruit and nut trees in Afghanistan and provide farmers there with the skills and support necessary for sustainable land use.

Manufactured in China by Insight Editions

10 9 8 7 6 5 4 3 2 1